THE COMPLETE BOOK OF
PATCHWORK
& QUILTING

Vincent & Rachel Hu
48th Dental Squadron
PSC 41 Box 1424
APO AE 09464

0/284   725726

Published in the UK 1992 by

Search Press Limited
Wellwood, North Farm Road,
Tunbridge Wells, Kent TN2 3DR

in association with

W. I. Books Ltd and Southgate Publishers Ltd
Glebe House, Church Street, Crediton,
Devon EX17 2AF

British Library Cataloguing in Publication Data
A CIP catalogue record for this book is available from
the British Library

Acknowledgements

Editor: Valerie Jackson
Managing Editor: Sue Parish
Designer: Clare Clements
Sub-editor: Gillian Andrews
Consultant: Pamela Allen
Contributor: Eleanor Allitt
Artists: Colin Salmon, Lindsay Blow, Vanessa Luff
All photographs except those on pages 12, 31, 61, 66,
75, 78, 102, 103 and 106 by Nick Nicholson

ISBN 0 85532 743 X

Printed and bound in Malaysia by Times Offset

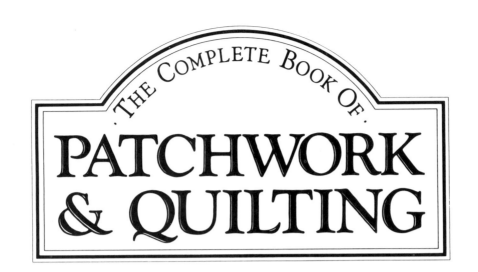

THE COMPLETE BOOK OF
PATCHWORK & QUILTING

SEARCH PRESS

Contents

Introduction 6
DESIGN AND COLOUR 8
PATCHWORK TECHNIQUES 28
QUILTING AND APPLIQUÉ 40
MAKING A QUILT 72
PATCHWORK VARIATIONS 86
SMALL THINGS TO MAKE 104
BEAUTIFUL QUILTS TO MAKE 118
Acknowledgements 156
Index 157

Foreword

When past WI Chairman Anne Harris wrote her original foreword to this book in 1985 she could scarcely have expected that within so short a time a third reprint would be needed to meet the popular demand for it from members and others. Many beginners and those more experienced must have been inspired already, just by leafing through the pages, to take up these skills or to adventure further. Through their interest, we can keep alive and hand down to future generations the crafts of our forebears which could otherwise so easily be lost.

The beautiful examples of quilts to be found here are a true reflection of the standard of work accomplished by WI members and I feel privileged to have been asked to write the foreword to what is one of our most sought-after books. Dig deep and you will find many useful tips and hints from experts as well as the secrets of making colours and shapes work with each other to bring end results of which you will be justly proud.

Through joining the WI, opportunities to learn traditional crafts are abundant. There are courses for both quilting and patchwork at Denman College, our own adult education establishment, and these courses, as well as many others, are today as popular as ever. Whether you choose to go on such a course or simply intend to put your skills to good use at home, treasure this book, for as a work of reference and as a showpiece for WI achievement, it is in a league of its own.

If you are not already a member of the WI but are interested in learning more, write to us at the National Federation of Women's Institutes, 104 New Kings Road, London SW6 4LY, or telephone 071 371 9300, and we will put you in touch with WIs near you, or similar organisations in your own country.

Susan Stockley
Chairman, NFWI
1992

Introduction

Some people think of patchwork as pieced or "English" patchwork, in which pieces of used fabric are cut into geometric or irregular shapes and joined together to make a mosaic surface of colored materials. Patchwork also means the stitching together of repeating squares of fabric, made up of pieced geometric shapes, a style particularly characteristic of the U.S. It can also be patched or "applied" work – the creation of designs by means of sewing fabric shapes onto a contrasting background. Many quilt patterns successfully combine patchwork and appliqué.

Patchwork of all kinds has been practiced for centuries, probably starting with pieced bedcovers, including applied and mosaic patchwork. Doubtless plenty of patchwork clothing was made too, but much of the work that survives from those early days dates from after the middle of the eighteenth century and has come down to us in the form of bedcovers. These often included quilting (an extra layer of padding sandwiched between top and backing with close stitching) so that the word "quilt" has become synonymous with "bedcover". Confusion sometimes arises from the fact that the word quilt describes bedcovers that are quilted layers of plain fabric, not pieced at all, and quilting of this kind also has a long tradition of its own both in the U.K. and in the U.S.

Whereas earlier needleworkers had made patchwork for the sake of economy, by the nineteenth century when cottons were cheap, plentiful and pretty, patchwork had become a fashionable pastime and in the Victorian and Edwardian periods was used to make all kinds of furnishings and took on fanciful forms such as "crazy work" (random pieces joined with decorative stitching).

Apart from a small revival in the 1930s, the fashion for patchwork faded away after World War One, but it is enjoying a renewed popularity now, not so much through a need to make use of old fabrics, though many people do enjoy the challenge of recycling, but as a satisfying and creative hobby that is often also a group activity.

Much of this revival of interest is due to the interchange of ideas with America, where quilting has been part of home and social life since settlers left Europe to found the New World. Because of the difficulty of obtaining supplies of fabric in a non-industrial society, families had to make use of every scrap of cloth they had brought with them. Long winters and few outside amusements established patchwork and communal quilting as a means of passing the time in a convivial yet useful way. The top of a bedcover would be made during the winter and quilting saved for the summer, when the cumbersome quilting frame could be set up outside. It could take one worker weeks to complete the quilting of a top, but if the neighbors joined in, it could be completed quite quickly. Then there would probably be a party to celebrate the occasion, whether it was an engagement, a twenty-first birthday or the presentation of a "friendship" quilt.

At first, housewives of the New World used the patterns they had learned in their native lands and these were passed down through the family, each generation of daughters adding to them. Hundreds of named designs were evolved which, when copied elsewhere, were often re-named, somewhat to our confusion! Some patterns stand for great historic occasions, others for family or social events, still others were inspired by the countryside and the religious beliefs of the settlers. It seems that now the wheel has turned full circle, for these well-loved designs are returning, enriched, to the continent that originated them.

The techniques required for patchwork, quilting and appliqué are not difficult to learn, and the satisfaction of making something useful and beautiful out of everyday materials is not the only reward for hours of patient stitching, for they are pleasant and soothing occupations in themselves. Making a quilt was always a creative outlet for women in an age when not many such outlets were available and now it offers an opportunity to explore the artistic possibilities of shape and colour in fabric as never before, for new cotton fabrics are readily obtainable and relatively inexpensive.

Patchwork enthusiasts and quilters are catered to by manufacturers on a scale which would have amazed and delighted our foremothers. Lovely fabrics printed in thousands of exciting colours and patterns, starter kits, pre-cut fabrics, Terylene wadding, coloured sheeting in generous widths for lining, and innovative sewing aids such as the non-woven, iron-on patchwork patterns printed with cut-and-stitch lines, all help to encourage beginners.

Although this book has been planned mainly with beginners in mind, experienced needleworkers will find much that is useful here. The first chapter, written by a teacher of patchwork and quilting, gives information on how to make colours and shapes work with each other. Chapter two contains template shapes for patchwork as well as basic techniques of the craft, and chapter three contains patterns for quilting as well as instructions on what you need for it and how to quilt. As group quilting is popular, chapter four has a section on how to go about this and for those who wish to experiment with other types of patchwork (such as log cabin or cathedral window), instructions will be found in chapter five. Chapter seven contains detailed instructions for making quilts designed by members of the Women's Institute in the U.K. and throughout the book you will find many helpful tips and hints from experts. In chapter six there are photographs of other, smaller items of clothing and ornaments to inspire those who would like to make something but find the prospect of a large piece of patchwork or quilting rather daunting.

Measurements given for the WI quilts in chapter seven are on the generous side to ensure that anyone wishing to make them will have sufficient materials. A ¼in (6mm) seam allowance is usually given, except in the instructions for some of the WI quilts, where more is allowed and in the instructions for making log cabin patchwork, where a seam allowance of 0.5cm is given, which was necessary here to make the metric measurement add up correctly.

Readers will see that we have given both Imperial and metric measurements throughout the book and you can work in either system, but as it is difficult to convert from one to the other with any degree of accuracy, be sure to use either Imperial or metric measurements. Do not try to mix the two.

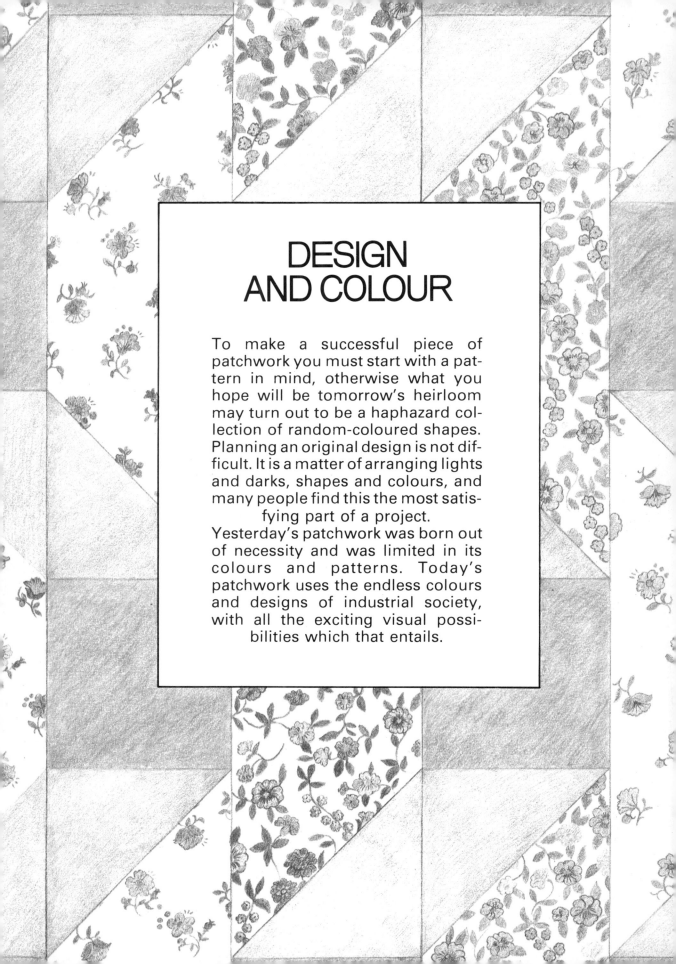

DESIGN
AND COLOUR

To make a successful piece of patchwork you must start with a pattern in mind, otherwise what you hope will be tomorrow's heirloom may turn out to be a haphazard collection of random-coloured shapes. Planning an original design is not difficult. It is a matter of arranging lights and darks, shapes and colours, and many people find this the most satisfying part of a project.

Yesterday's patchwork was born out of necessity and was limited in its colours and patterns. Today's patchwork uses the endless colours and designs of industrial society, with all the exciting visual possibilities which that entails.

The planning stage

When planning a bedcover, remember that a bed is the largest item in a room, and so the background colour of the quilt will dominate any other colour scheme.

Plan the design to suit the room. A bold abstract design would look out of place in a "period" room and conversely, a floral chintz would look strange in a very modern room.

The planning stage of making any piece of patchwork is very important, for its success or failure depends on it. You may be consumed with desire to start work at once with needle, thread and scissors but as the patchwork may well last for several generations, it makes sense to spend time and thought on the design.

Design means planning and it involves asking yourself a series of questions about shape, tone and colour and finding the answers to them. This chapter pinpoints the problems you need to consider and suggests how to arrive at the answers.

One of the first things to think about is the setting. What colour are the curtains, carpet and furniture of the room in which the patchwork is to go? What is the patchwork intended for: a bed, a cushion or a wall-hanging?

Think next about dimensions. If it is for a bed, does the bed have a headboard? What size is the bed? Measure it, allowing a 12in–18in (30cm–46cm) overhang each side and top and bottom but omitting these last overhangs if there are head and tailboards. At the corners the quilt will hang in folds, which is a pleasing feature, though you may prefer the traditional quilt design in which squares are cut out of the bottom two corners.

Colour, too, needs careful thought. What overall colour scheme do you want for your patchwork? Do you want it to blend in with the colour of the room for which it is planned or would it be more exciting to provide a contrast? A quilt can form a dramatic focal point for a drab room. The early Americans had few rich or colourful possessions and their quilts provided interest in rooms which would otherwise have been very stark.

Further considerations concern fabrics. Remember that it is never worthwhile using old or worn fabrics, as they may go to pieces in the first wash. If you do use old scraps, use those in good condition, cutting out the seamed bits and making sure they are colourfast and pre-shrunk. Buy the best new fabrics you can afford and when buying take with you a swatch of the colour scheme you have in mind.

The patterns you choose will depend a good deal on the shapes you will be using. In general, small designs work better than bold ones but there are exceptions to this rule. You can often use a bold design to override a formal geometric structure. In the quilt shown on page 12 for example, you will notice that the hexagon shapes are subordinate to the main design.

Having begun to think about some of the questions that need to be answered before starting, look at other quilts, old and new, to see how other quiltmakers have solved the same problems. Many museums have wonderful collections of old quilts, some on display, others available on request to study groups. It is well worth joining a group of quiltmakers, not only for visits such as this but to share knowledge and to join in quilting "workshops" and other events.

Borrow or buy books on quiltmaking. Look at pictures of tiles, mosaic floors, wallpapers, textiles and rugs and think how their designs can be adapted.

A room can be transformed by a brightly coloured quilt. (By Shipton Oliffe WI).

Choosing the shapes

Decide what shapes you want to use. Nearly all patchwork is made from repeating units, which may be a single shape such as the hexagon or diamond so typical of English patchwork, or a series of repeating shapes as in American block patchwork. The secret of planning is to limit the shapes: for example, just hexagons or a single block design. This will give you greater freedom in your choice of colour later.

Draw the chosen shapes on graph paper to see how they will fit together in the quilt you have in mind.

Sheila Yale's "Star" quilt demonstrates the skilful use of hexagons.

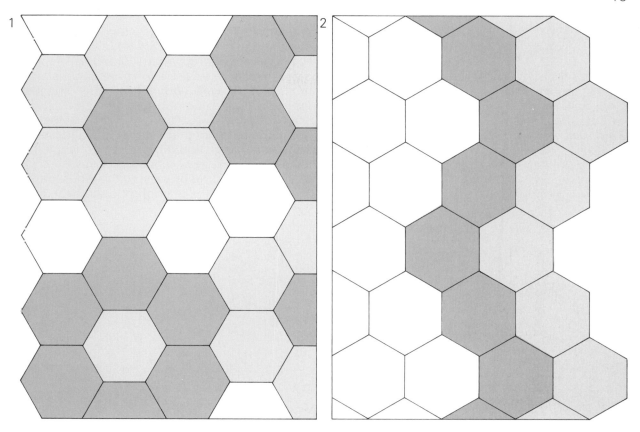

Hexagons

These six-sided shapes with equal sides and angles, much loved by beginners, can be used on their own in patchwork or be combined with the short diamonds (lozenges).

Hexagons can also be used as borders by arranging them in straight strips (1), or in wavy strips with an irregular edge, known as the "ocean wave" pattern (2).

The hexagon pattern known as "grandmother's flower garden", or "rosette" (3) (centre of design), is the simplest hexagon grouping. It is made up of 6, 12 or 18 equilateral hexagon patches joined together around a central hexagon patch and it is seen on some of the oldest patchwork quilts. It is used either as a single motif or to form units in a larger pattern of hexagons or of hexagons and diamonds.

The central rosette can be turned into a lozenge-shaped block (3) by adding extra hexagons (shown in dotted lines) on opposite sides of the main block. This too can be used either as a single motif or to form a unit in a larger pattern.

Draw out hexagons on isometric graph paper (graph paper set out in triangles) into which they fit neatly. There is no need to draw out each hexagon in your plan but it is important to plan out the general arrangement to find out how many hexagon blocks or rosettes will be needed and how they will fit into the finished quilt size. To do this, decide on the size of each hexagon and consequently of each rosette. Do not choose a small size unless you enjoy fussy work. If the hexagon sides measure 1½in (4cm), this is a comfortable size with which to start.

Hexagons, forming a straight edge (1), "ocean wave" edging (2), and (3) "grandmother's flower garden" and a lozenge shape.

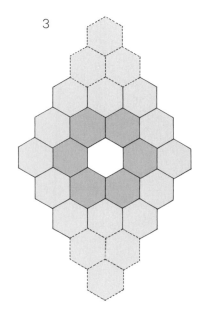

Diamonds

The diamond shape is a great favourite with quilters. Perhaps the best-known diamond design is "baby blocks" (1) (also known as "tumbling blocks"), the eye-deceiving pattern composed of three diamonds put together to resemble a series of three-dimensional cubes. But diamonds also fit well with many other shapes: octagons, hexagons and triangles among them.

The lozenge diamond (2), made up of two equilateral triangles, does not fit happily into the ordinary graph paper grid and, as for the hexagon, accurate templates should be drawn on isometric graph paper or they should be drawn with compasses.

Diamonds can be made interesting by varying the tones (darks and lights), by varying the sizes of the diamonds, or both (3), also

1 A three-diamond "baby blocks" design.
2 An arrangement of light and dark lozenge diamonds.
3 A design of small diamonds enlivened by large ones.
4 Dark diamonds, with strips of triangles, and light diamonds placed on their sides.

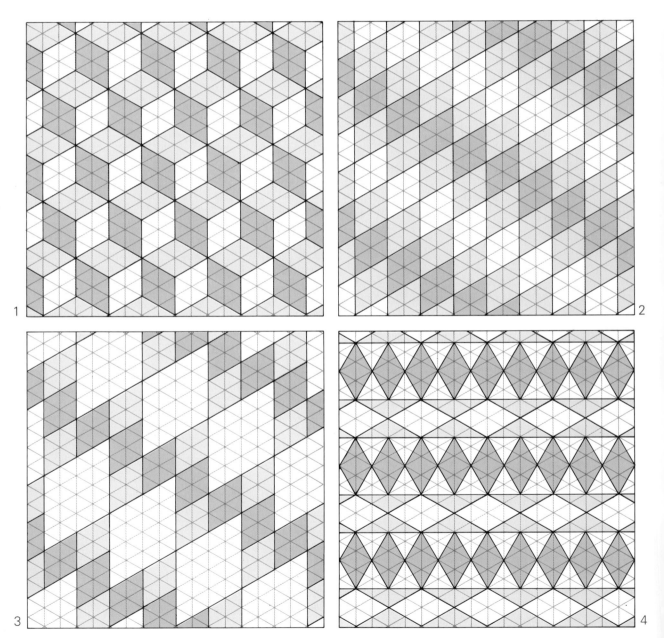

by turning some diamonds on their sides and interspersing them with triangles (4).

Diamonds go well with rhomboids (5), and if you place darks and lights correctly, they can take on a three-dimensional effect as in "baby blocks". They also fit with long hexagons (6).

Stars

Stars can be formed from six diamonds, when they are a development of the hexagon shape (7), or they can be eight-pointed. Eight-pointed stars are a development of the square and they are constructed from eight long diamonds (8). They form the basis of many beautiful block designs including the famous "star of Bethlehem".

5 A three-dimensional design of diamonds and rhomboids.
6 Diamonds and long hexagons.
7 A six-pointed star, made from six diamonds.
8 An eight-pointed star, made from eight long diamonds.

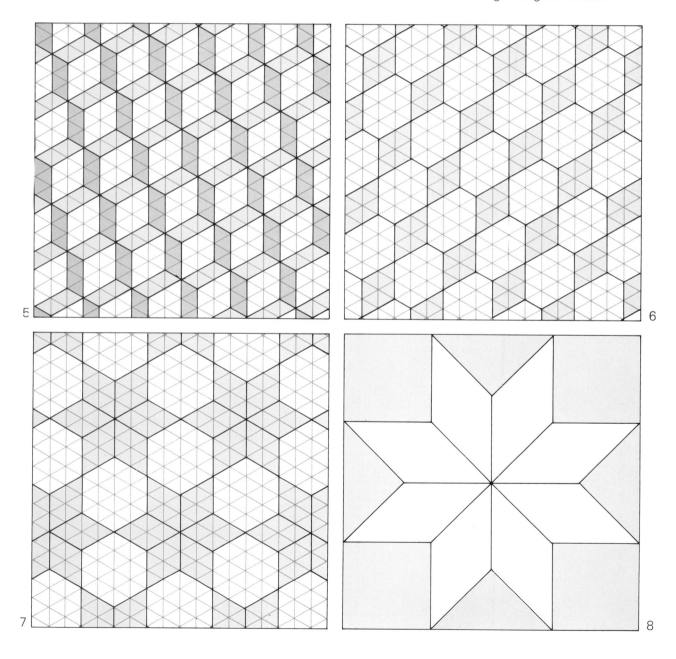

5

6

7

8

Triangles

Triangles are versatile shapes, combining with squares, hexagons, diamonds and rhomboids (1) to make an almost infinite variety of patterns. The equilateral triangle has all its sides of equal length and is made by halving a diamond widthways. It is the basis of the well-known "pyramids" design (2). There is also the isosceles triangle, with two sides of equal length, which can be made by cutting a square diagonally, or by halving a diamond lengthways.

Squares and rectangles

Many variations of pattern can be achieved by arranging squares in light, medium and dark shades, and some patchwork designs

1 Equilateral triangles and rhomboids.
2 "Pyramids" design.
3 Large and small squares.
4 Squares set diagonally to form squat diamonds.

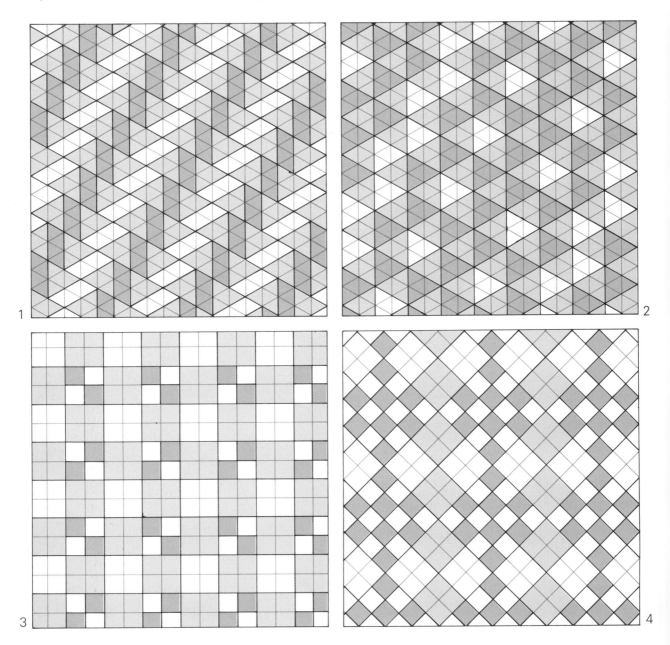

are based on the square alone (3). However, it can be a little dull on its own and it is more often used with other shapes such as the octagon, triangle, long hexagon and rectangle. Squares placed diagonally form squat diamonds (4).

The two traditional designs based on rectangles are the "brick wall", and a zigzag made by placing the rectangles in diagonal blocks so that their ends form triangles (6), but rectangles are not often used on their own. Variations of pattern can be made using two tones, and rectangles also team up with squares and the shapes used with squares. The rhomboid (parallelogram) is an adaptation of the rectangle.

Several different designs can be made by mixing squares and rectangles without the addition of other shapes (7 and 8).

5 A variation of "brick wall" using squares and rectangles.
6 A zigzag pattern of rectangles.
7 and 8 Two ways of using squares and rectangles.

Right: The design of this quilt depends on the placing of dark shapes on a light background. By Eleanor Allitt.
Below: a wall-hanging made with six different arrangements of the same tones and colours. By Muriel Tooby.

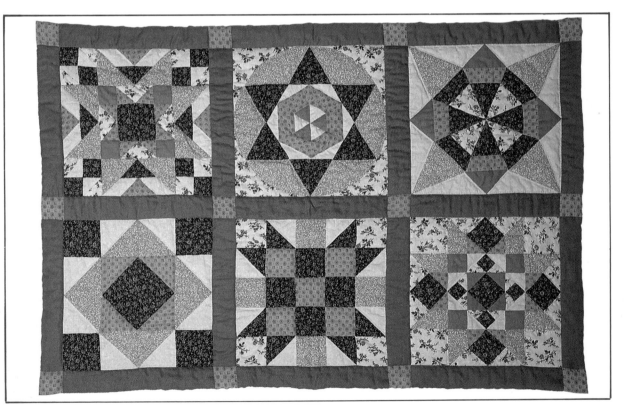

The importance of tones

Every design depends for its impact on contrast of one sort or another, and there are many ways of achieving this with contrasting shapes, colours, textures and, most important of all in patchwork, with contrasting tones.

Tone is the term used to describe the amount of lightness or darkness in colour and it is essential to the success of any patchwork to plan the tones, otherwise the finished effect will be a jumble of colours and shapes which do not enrich each other.

If you look at the first picture on the opposite page through half-closed eyes, you will notice that the black vertical lines of diamonds and the strips of dark green are much darker in tone than all the other colours and so provide a contrast to the background colours. These are all in similar, lighter tones and so serve to set off the dark colours. Squinting through half-closed eyes is one way to see different tones clearly without the distraction of colour. Another way is to look through a piece of dark glass.

In the "green diamond" quilt on page 25, the tones which stand out and contrast with the others are the very light ones, and here the whites are emphasized by the darker colours.

Tone influences the overall pattern of all designs. This is particularly noticeable in log cabin patchwork, where the patchwork shapes themselves are less important than the way the light and dark tones are arranged. The well-known "barn raising" design forms a pattern of dark diagonals on a light ground and another log cabin design called "courthouse steps" forms strips of dark hourglass shapes on a light ground (see pages 88–91).

Tones can also form optical illusions, as in the "baby blocks" design, where three diamonds of different tones are put together so that they look like cubes. A strip of alternating dark and light rhomboids gives the effect of concertina-folded paper.

Different arrangements of the same tones and colours will change the effect of those tones and colours completely. The bottom photograph opposite shows a wall-hanging in which the same five tones and colours have been used on six different block patterns, and it is interesting to see how these tones and colours behave in their different settings. Conversely, the wall-hangings on page 24 were both made from the same block pattern but they look very different because other parts of the design have been emphasized by the varying tones and colours.

Try this out by making an uncomplicated block design on squared paper then repeating it several times, colouring each block in different tones. You will see that other designs will emerge. Books containing full-page drawings of repeating blocks are available and you can learn a great deal by experimenting with these to find out how many patterns can be made from the same basic design. It is only by planning like this that the colours will work as a team to help each other.

When working out the shapes for patchwork, it is best to use pencil and biro rather than coloured crayons or felt-tipped pens. The dark biro, medium-toned pencil and white paper will give you three tones, without the distraction of colour.

This dark, shading-to-light block shows different tones from black to white.

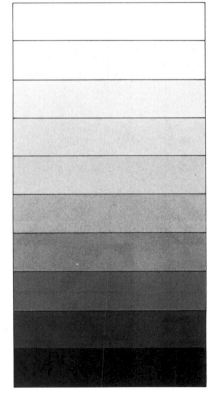

American block patterns

When designing a block pattern, you can get a completely different effect with precisely the same fabrics and the same patterns, by changing their positions on the block.

Design blocks the size of the *finished* block. Do not add seam allowances until the template stage; then add the seam allowances all around the sides of all the pieces.

Block patterns, which are slightly more complex repeating shapes than those on the preceding pages, are generally used on bed quilts. Each block consists of a square composed of several shapes, and several blocks join together to make an overall repeating design. There are basically two kinds of blocks: symmetrical, in which both halves of the block are identical, and asymmetrical (such as "flower basket") in which the halves differ. Asymmetrical blocks often form a quarter of a design which needs three more blocks to complete it.

Complicated though it looks, the traditional "flower basket" design is made of only three different shapes: a rectangle, a large triangle and a small triangle, all fitted into a grid of four squares by four squares. A grid is the number of squares into which a pattern will divide equally and it can be two, three, five, seven or multiples of these numbers. On the opposite page are examples of three-, four- and five-square grids.

To compose your own block, outline your chosen grid on squared paper and draw some shapes within the grid. Stick to not more than three simple shapes to begin with, and avoid curves. Sketch medium and dark tones in some of the shapes.

To see how the design will look when it is repeated, place two handbag mirrors vertical to the diagram along two adjacent edges of the block. The blocks and the new shapes they make when they are put together will be reflected in the mirrors.

Decide how big each block is to be. The average block size is about 10in (25cm) but will depend on the size of the bed and how much is needed for overhang. Adjust the border size (and therefore the finished quilt size) to fit in with the number of blocks you plan, or round the dimensions of the quilt up or round down and eliminate the border, or adjust the size of the blocks until they fit.

Some of the blocks can be squares of printed or plain fabric and lattice strips can also increase the size of a quilt (see overleaf). Work out how many blocks you need, then make an accurate scale drawing of your block on squared paper, from which to make templates later and from which to calculate the number of patches needed of each colour.

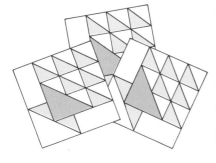

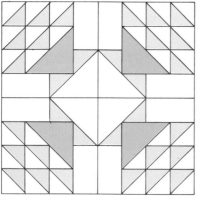
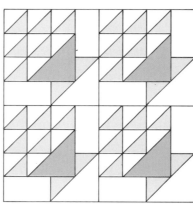
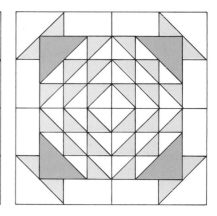

Different arrangements of four "flower basket" designs.

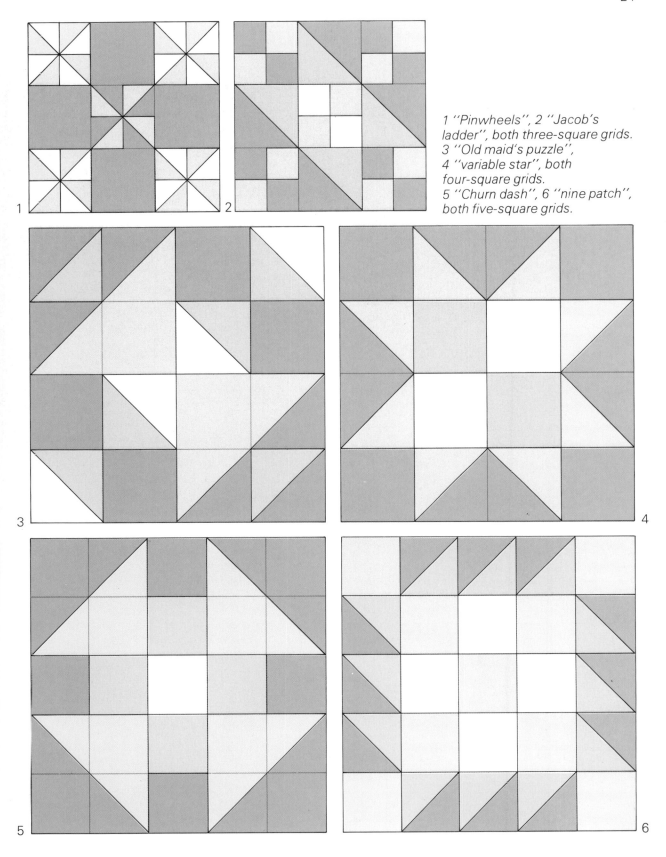

1 "Pinwheels", 2 "Jacob's ladder", both three-square grids. 3 "Old maid's puzzle", 4 "variable star", both four-square grids. 5 "Churn dash", 6 "nine patch", both five-square grids.

1 "Handy Andy", a five-square grid.
2 "Cats and mice", 3 "sky rocket", both six-square grids.
4 "Bear's paw", 5 "prickly pear", 6 "hens and chickens", all seven-square grids.

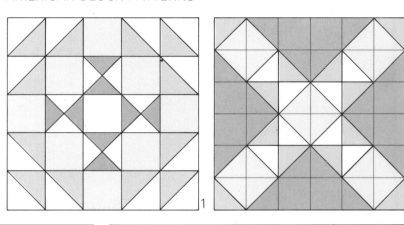

Lattices and borders

Lattices, otherwise called lattice strips, lattice bands or sashings, are long bands of plain, patterned or patchwork fabric which separate the blocks. You can have vertical lattices only or horizontal lattices only: they do not necessarily have to go all around the blocks.

Lattices can make a quilt larger without too much expenditure of time and they can unify the various colours, something which is often necessary in a scrap quilt.

Not all designs call for lattices. Blocks can adjoin each other, or be interspersed with printed or plain or quilted fabric blocks. To lessen the impact of lattices, you can make them the same tone as the blocks.

Borders

A border is the "picture frame" for a quilt and it can also serve the practical purpose of making a quilt larger. Some people like to plan a border right from the beginning; others prefer to wait until the main part of the quilt has been made, as by then they have discovered how the colours and shapes work together, but whichever way you plan it, the border is an important part of the finished work.

Borders can contrast or blend in with the main panel. They can be in bands of colour, or plain, or in patterned fabric or in patchwork. If they are in patterned fabric or in patchwork, the pattern must turn the corners satisfactorily. Design borders on squared paper to ensure that they fit.

Traditional patchwork border designs include rectangles, triangles, squares, chevrons and other geometric shapes. Sometimes two or more different patchwork borders are stitched around a single central motif.

1 Design for a patchwork border or lattice strip.
2 Corner section of a patchwork border.

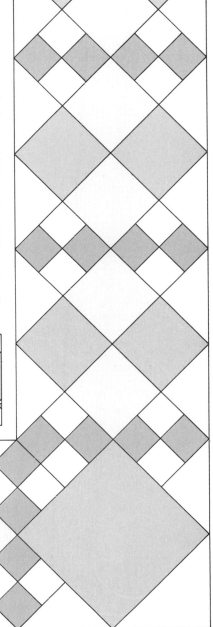

1

2

Colour schemes

When deciding what colours to use, it helps to keep your fabrics in colour "families", so that all the reds are together, all the blues are together and so on. Then when you want to try one colour against another, you will not have to search through a kaleidoscope of fabrics to find the one you need.

Colours take on different characteristics when placed in different settings, which can make for some exciting schemes. For example, pale blue is intensified by bright red, viridian green by dark purple. A roll or length of fabric will look a different colour when it is cut up into small pieces and placed next to other colours. In view of the unexpected ways in which colours can behave in different contexts, after deciding on a general colour scheme it is best to work directly with the fabric you intend to use.

Two wall-hangings in the same design but in different colours, by Eleanor Allitt.

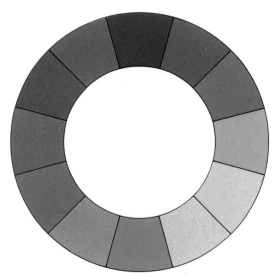

A safe colour recipe for beginners is to use shades of one colour from one side of the colour wheel with a small accent of colour from the opposite side. Try not to be timid about colour. A quilt with no colour accents would be a dull one.

To see how the colour principle works, it helps to look at a colour circle, to see how colours are related to each other. There are three primary colours: red, yellow and blue. All other colours are made by mixing these primaries.

Secondary colours are made by mixing two primary colours. Equal parts of red and yellow make the secondary colour, orange; equal parts of yellow and blue make green; equal parts of blue and red make mauve.

On the circle, the primary colours merge into the secondary colours and back to primary colours, each group of colours forming a "family". When painting, each colour in the circle can be mixed with its near neighbours, its middle distant neighbours and its opposites, as well as with black and white, in infinitely varying proportions.

The colour wheel is useful for planning colour schemes. If you take a group of colours from one family and lay your ruler on the circle from the centre of this group through the centre of the circle to the opposite side, you will find a colour which will make a good contrast. This is known as a "complementary" colour.

Two complementary colours of the same intensity placed side by side have a powerful effect on each other but on the whole, a contrasting colour should be in small proportion to the chosen colour family.

Unrelated colours can be brought into harmony with each other by the influence of one major colour, an effect which is seen by looking at a group of colours through coloured glass. You can achieve the same effect with fabrics by over-dyeing them, which will give you a collection of colour-related fabrics. They will come out of the dye bath in different but harmonious colours, newly related by the colour in which they have been dipped.

Some patchworks are based on colours taken entirely from one colour family, in different tones and tints of one basic colour. This can look pleasing, though it can also be rather dull and it is often better to work with more than one colour family, introducing a small quantity of an opposing colour to set off the others.

Always have one dominant colour or colour family in your patchwork to act as an anchor for the less dominant colours.

The mainly green colours of the quilt in the photograph above are made more interesting by the occasional use of brown. By Eleanor Allitt.

Adding extra interest

After drawing a sketch plan, put all possible patchwork fabrics in a pile on a white sheet; then select suitable ones in tones that relate to your drawing. Cut rough shapes from the selected fabrics to match the shapes in the plan and arrange them on a white background.

Possible colour combinations are something to think about at this stage. Many of the most beautiful early American quilts are based on two colours only, such as Turkey red and white. Equally effective is blue and white, or blue and white with a small quantity of contrasting colour. As a variation, try a single colour with beige, grey or black instead of white for a good contrast of colour and tone.

Three colours, such as pink and green on white, or grey and pink on white also make good colour schemes. Grey, red and black, or red, blue and black sound unlikely colour partners, yet modern quilters have used them together successfully.

Four colours give you still more scope. In the quilt on the opposite page there are four reds, one beige, one natural and one green. The dark red diamond centres and the natural unbleached calico provide the tonal contrast and the green provides the colour contrast.

The use of white on white is another interesting variation to try, in which two shades of white are used next to each other to give an exciting sparkle to a colour scheme. This is illustrated in the photograph of the green quilt on the previous page, where white piqué and unbleached calico were used side by side.

Resting areas
Patchwork items made entirely from patterned fabric are rarely successful. Exceptions to this are when the patterns are unobtrusive or when they are subordinated to the general design, but usually the effect is "busy" and confused. Areas of plain fabric act as visual "resting" areas, as a quiet contrast to the busy patterns. A glance at the illustrations in this book will show how important they are.

Texture
Texture adds variety, interest and fun to patchwork. Examples of textured fabric are those with unusual surfaces like seersucker, broderie anglaise, wool and lace. You can also use couched wool, netting, ribbons, raised machine-stitched seams, tucking, piping, buttons, tassels and raw edges, though you have to be a little careful what you include in a quilt, which has to be washed often in its lifetime. Quilting creates yet another surface effect, and it goes very well with patchwork.

Stencilling
Cutting a stencil and spraying through it with fabric dye to fit an area that needs extra pattern is a technique with possibilities. A stencilled panel makes a pleasant contrast to a plain one.

Informal shapes
It is sometimes effective to break up a formal geometric shape by sewing random-length pieced strips within it. This is illustrated by the green quilt on the previous page, where the diamonds are bounded by formal shapes that contain pieced fabric strips.

A four-colour quilt in reds, beige, natural and green, by Eleanor Allitt.

PATCHWORK TECHNIQUES

Once you have decided what you wish to make in patchwork, sketched out a design for it and bought or otherwise obtained the fabrics, you can choose one of three different methods for putting the patches together: by hand, using paper templates; by hand, without paper templates; or by machine, also without paper templates.

Whichever method you use, you will need to cut out accurate shapes in fabric and paper and sew them together precisely.

The beauty of patchwork depends on accuracy and the skilful alignment of patches, as well as on the choice of pleasing colours and shapes.

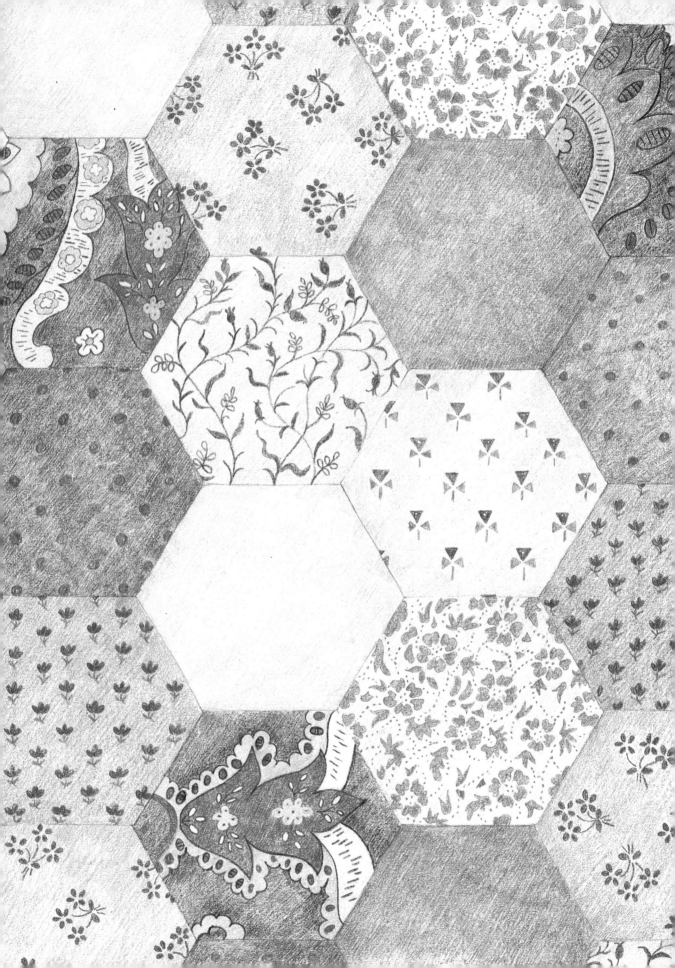

What you need

Fabrics

Patchwork fabrics must always be of similar weight and type. They should not be too thick but they should be firmly woven to avoid fraying and stretching. The larger the item, the thicker the fabric can be.

Fabrics should be colourfast. If in doubt, test the fabric before using by immersing it in a bowl of warm water and leaving it there overnight. If the colour runs, change the water until it is free of dye, then drip-dry and iron on the wrong side.

Washable fabrics should in any case be washed before using them for patchwork because some shrink more than others and this could cause the finished item to pucker. Try not to mix natural and synthetic fabrics as the fibres have different sewing and laundering requirements.

Cottons mixed with synthetic fibres are strong and crease-resistant but crease resistance is not an advantage in patchwork, where a crisp fold is needed for accuracy. Test cotton/synthetic mixtures for their non-fray seaming and creasing properties.

Dress prints, poplin, shirting, chintz, denim, good quality gingham, silk, piqué and fine linen are all good fabrics for patchwork.

Needles

Use fine needles, about size nine or ten, for small stitches (the larger the number the smaller the needle), and a larger needle for tacking. However, the needle size is really a matter of personal preference. Use sharp needles for machine-sewing.

Scissors

You need three sharp pairs. One for cutting out fabric patches, embroidery scissors for snipping off thread ends and for fine work, and a pair for cutting paper templates, as paper-cutting blunts dressmaking scissors faster than almost anything.

Pins

Use fine pins; coarse ones will mark most fabrics.

Thread

Use fine sewing thread in the predominant colour of the patchwork. Match the type of thread to the type of fabric. When sewing a lot of different colours together, choose a neutral shade, but if you are sewing two colours, dark and light, match the thread to the darker colour.

Thimble

A thimble on your middle finger enables you to sew with an even rhythm and prevents the finger that is doing the pushing from getting sore.

Lead pencil

This is used for marking out the fabric patches on the wrong side. Use a B grade. Do not use a ballpoint or a felt-tipped pen, as these will make permanent marks on the fabric.

Thick paper

Thick paper or thin cardboard, such as old Christmas cards or brochures, is an ideal thickness for templates. Do not use cardboard thicker than this as it will be too thick for the needle to penetrate. Test to make sure that the ink or dye on the printed card does not smudge before using.

Metal and plastic templates can be bought in many sizes and shapes. It is useful to buy them in a set, the same size, with matching window templates which can be laid on the right side of the fabric to show the effect of a finished patch. Window templates are an extra ¼ in (6mm) bigger all around than solid templates to allow for turnings. Solid templates represent the finished size of the finished patch and they are the patterns from which card patterns are cut. You can make your own templates out of thin cardboard or thick stencil paper or fine sandpaper.

Templates

A thick cork board or a piece of firm polystyrene is useful. You can pin patches on it while planning the design, to see the effect.

Board

Designs based on squares and rectangles can be worked out on graph paper with coloured felt-tipped pens or with crayons. To enlarge such designs, you can use the squared paper sold for dressmaking patterns. (See page 50 for enlarging designs.)

Graph paper

Designs based on hexagons and diamonds can be worked out on the isometric paper sold by draughtsmens' suppliers. Enlarge designs by using larger numbers of sections of the paper.

Isometric paper

"Medallion" patchwork quilt by Pamela Dempster.

Patchwork templates

Long diamond

Short diamond

On these pages and overleaf you will find some useful template shapes for patchwork. Most of them have been drawn in 2in (5cm), 1½in (3cm) and 1in (2.5cm) sizes ready for tracing. No seam allowances have been given on any of these shapes, so remember to add an extra ¼in (6mm) all around each one when you are using them to cut out the fabric shapes.

Coffin

Hexagon

Church window

Irregular pentagon

Clamshell

Isosceles triangle

Equilateral triangle

Right-angled triangle

Octagon

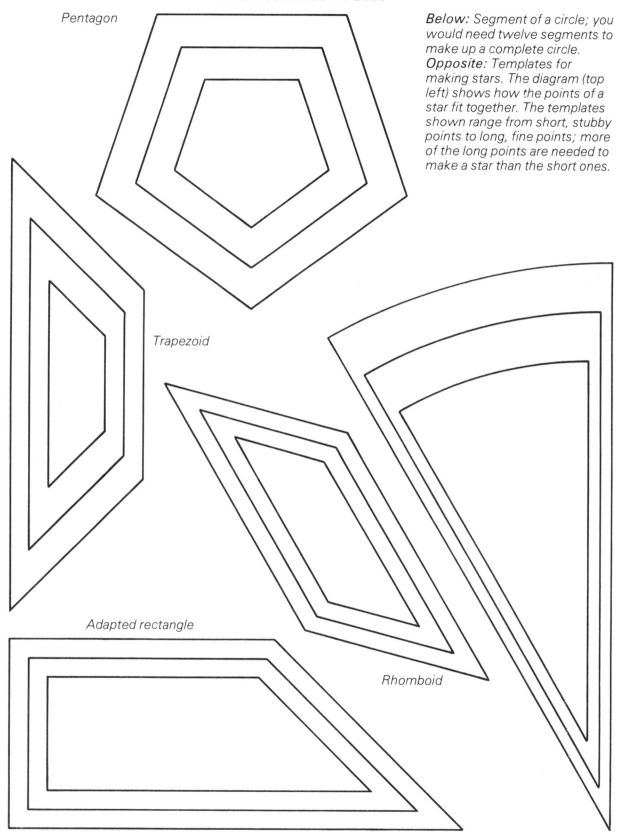

Pentagon

Below: Segment of a circle; you would need twelve segments to make up a complete circle.
Opposite: Templates for making stars. The diagram (top left) shows how the points of a star fit together. The templates shown range from short, stubby points to long, fine points; more of the long points are needed to make a star than the short ones.

Trapezoid

Adapted rectangle

Rhomboid

Sewing patchwork

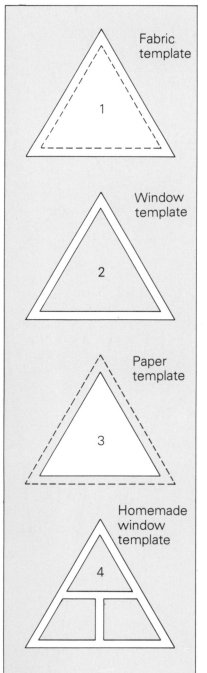

Fabric template

1

Window template

2

Paper template

3

Homemade window template

4

Hand patchwork using paper templates

Templates are bought as a set of two, one made to the exact size of the finished patch, for cutting paper templates (3), and one a "window" template, ¼in (6mm) larger all around than the first, to enable you to see what the finished patch will look like (2). For hand-sewing with papers, a third template can be useful. This is the same size as the window template, but solid, and is for cutting fabric with a seam allowance included (1).

You can make your own templates, but they must be accurate. Draw them on graph paper when possible, then cut them out and stick them on firm cardboard or fine sandpaper (which will pre-vent them from slipping when you cut the fabric).

When making any kind of template, accuracy is all-important, for even the smallest deviation from the correct shape will cause problems during making up. If using home-made cardboard templates, do not over-use them, as they will go out of shape. Check them with a ruler from time to time.

Template 1, which is ¼in (6mm) bigger on all sides than the finished patch, is used for cutting most fabrics, i.e. plain fabrics and those with very small patterns. Cut enough patches for a section of your design and pin them to a board in the arrange-ment you have chosen.

Template 2 is a window template. It also has the extra ¼in (6mm) seam allowance all around and it allows you to see clearly where the pattern will fall on the finished patch. When you have chosen the section of fabric you wish to use, mark the fabric (on the right side) in pencil, drawing around the *outer* edges of the window template. Cut out the fabric on the pencil line.

Make sure homemade window templates do not bend out of shape as you draw around them. Hold them firmly while drawing or leave some areas uncut to strengthen them (4).

Cut enough patches for a small section of your design and pin them to a board, as for template 1.

Template 3 is the size of the finished patch and it is used to cut paper linings for patches. When making paper templates, don't draw around them in pencil before cutting out, as this makes for inaccuracy. Instead, hold the paper and template together firmly so they do not slip, then cut out the paper with the scissors' blade close to the contours of the templates. Cut beyond each point before cutting the next side of the shape. Try to make only one cut for each side of a shape and do not cut out more than two paper patterns at a time.

Paper templates can also be cut with a sharp craft knife on a board. Cut enough shapes to make a section of a design and store the shapes flat.

When drawing around templates on fabric, draw in soft pencil, on the outside of the template for the cutting line, and, if you wish, on the inside of the window template for the sewing line but remember to do this on the *wrong* side of the fabric. Do not press too hard, or the pencil will drag the fabric.

Hand patchwork without papers

Window templates are used for hand-sewing without papers. The inside edge of the window template is the sewing line and the size of the finished patch, while the outside edge is the fabric cutting line. Mark the sewing line on the wrong side of the fabric in pencil, then cut out on the cutting line.

Sew the smallest pieces of a block together first, then the larger units and then the rows.

Do not press seams open. Either press towards the darkest fabric or, to prevent ridges forming on long stretches, press seams in alternate directions.

 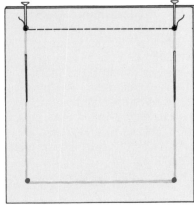 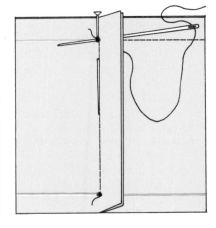

1 With right sides of patches facing each other and pencil lines matching, pin patches together. Pencil a dot at the ends of each sewing line and pin on dots.

2 Sew together with small running stitches, matching dots. Start and end each seam with a knot or backstitch. Make a backstitch every three or four stitches as you go along, for added strength.

3 Do not sew over the seam allowance but sew along the stitching line up to the first vertical seam, then make a backstitch and slip the needle through the seam allowance, ready to sew the next square in the row.

Machine-sewing

When making block patchwork, as in hand-sewing (above), use window templates to make the patches and sew the smallest pieces together first. Machine sewing is suitable for all but the smallest shapes, but patches must be cut accurately because the seam is guided by the presser foot, the width of which sets the seam allowance. If the presser foot is not the right width for a seam, stick a narrow strip of masking tape on the footplate to indicate the width required.

No tacking is necessary in machine-patchwork, as pieces can be pin-tacked, the pins perpendicular to the line being sewn, at all the joins. You can machine over the pins.

Save time when machine sewing by stitching together similar pieces of each block at the same time, assembly-line fashion. In this way, all the blocks will come to completion at the same time. This is known as "string sewing". Machine the pieces together one after the other without snipping the threads between, leaving this until you have a long strip of joined sections.

The zigzag stitch (on the *right* side of the fabric) can be used to good effect in machine sewing. It joins the patches quickly and gives a decorative finish. No seam allowance is required.

Sewing wide-angled shapes

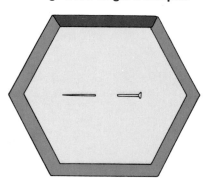

1 Place the paper template in the centre of the fabric patch on the wrong side of the fabric, two sides on the straight grain of the fabric. Pin if necessary to stop it slipping. Starting with a side of the shape on the straight of the fabric, fold seam allowance over the paper, making sure the fold lies tight up against the paper.

2 Begin tacking by taking a stitch through two thicknesses of fabric and one of paper, about one third of the way along the first side of the shape. If you make a knot to begin with, you can pull it out easily when taking out tacking stitches. Do not tack too finely.

3 Fold the fabric over the second side of the shape. Place a tacking stitch through the fold at the corner and bring the stitch up one third of the way along the second side. Continue like this around the patch, taking a tacking stitch from corner to corner until the patch is complete. Finish on the wrong side.

Sewing pointed shapes

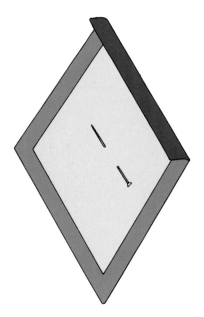

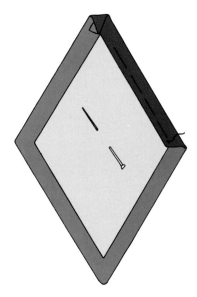

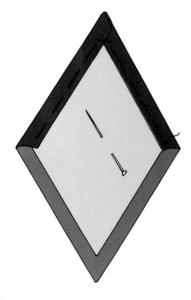

1 Lay the paper template in the centre of the fabric patch on the wrong side of the fabric, with two sides on the straight grain of the fabric. Fold the seam allowance over the paper making sure the fold lies tight up against the paper.

2 Begin tacking as shown and fold the fabric over at the top point so that the fold runs parallel to the edge of the paper but does not overlap it. Do not stitch this fold yet.

3 Fold the seam allowance with its folded point over the paper as shown and continue tacking. Repeat the double fold at the bottom point. Fold and tack the fourth side.

Sewing patchwork together

With a fine needle and fine thread, join hand-sewn patches by oversewing them on the wrong side. Try to avoid sewing through paper linings: if you do, it is difficult to remove them when work is completed. Try to keep paper templates in place as long as possible; it helps to prevent the work stretching.

Squeeze the fabric together away from the papers as you sew. If you do this, you can make slightly larger stitches without fear of them showing.

Sew from the very beginning of a shape to its very end, leaving no gaps. Fasten off by oversewing back for 2in (5cm).

All seams, whether hand or machine sewn, must meet precisely. Plan joining sequences well in advance. Join smaller pieces to make bigger sections, join patches or blocks in straight strips, then join the strips to form still larger pieces. This is especially necessary when joining pointed pieces (see diagram, right). When working on shapes such as these, join strips from the centre to one end, matching seams, then work from the middle of the strip to the other end.

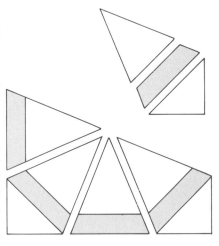

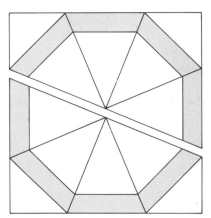

A typical joining sequence with pointed shapes. First join the smaller pieces, then join the larger pieces in a straight line. Then join the two straight pieces from the centre outwards.

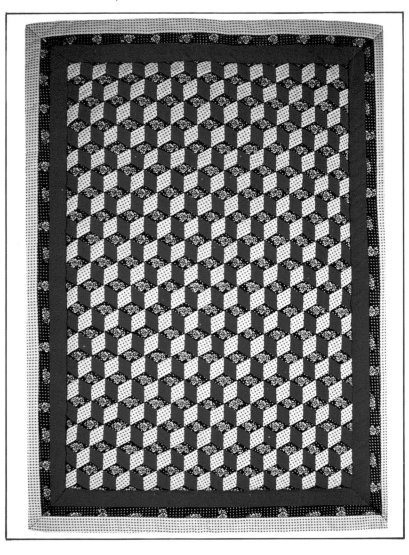

Left: "Tumbling blocks" quilt made by Preston On Stour WI, Warwicks.

QUILTING AND APPLIQUÉ

Quilting is defined as the stitching together of two pieces of cloth with soft padding material between them. Appliqué is the sewing of small cut-out pieces of fabric onto a large background piece.

Both these sewing methods can be used with patchwork and are especially useful techniques in the making of bedcovers – some of the quilts shown in this book demonstrate how effective they can be.

Quilting adds an attractive richness and texture to patchwork which make it well worth the extra time and trouble taken to do it, while appliqué designs give great scope for individual artistic expression.

The craft of quilting

Look out for useful sewing aids as they come on the market. Quilters may like the light, flexible leather thimble which is open at the top and has a small metal plate at the side to protect the finger from the blunt end of the needle.

Quilting and patchwork are crafts which complement each other perfectly and patchwork bedcovers have often been quilted in the past. Sometimes they were filled with an old blanket or a piece of flannel or, when times were hard, with corn husks, leaves or paper materials, which are now replaced by easily-washed synthetic wadding.

Synthetic wadding, which is also known as "batting" or "padding," comes in different thicknesses, but usually a light-weight wadding is used. Quilting is the fastening together of two layers of fabric with wadding between layers, secured either with knots or stitches.

The craft of quilting is a very old one. As we can see from museum collections, it has been used as a fashion accessory from time to time, and it was once worn by soldiers under their armour to prevent chafing or on top of it to deflect enemy arrows. But more importantly, people living in the colder climates of the world have always needed to keep warm, and sewing two or three layers of fabric together was, and still is, a very efficient form of insulation. As well as looking smart, a quilted petticoat or jacket would have been a great comfort in the draughty, unheated houses of our ancestors and a quilted bedcover would have been a most desirable, warm and decorative possession, prized even in the noblest of homes.

What started as a purely utilitarian craft, gradually became a decorative one. Stitches became finer and were made to form decorative scrolls, formalized flowers and other fanciful shapes. Neat rows of background quilting set off grand and complicated central motifs designed to demonstrate the quilter's skill. Quilting has become a folk art in its own right.

Types of quilting

There are several types of quilting. In Trapunto (stuffed) quilting, certain areas of a design are backed with a second layer of fabric, joined to the top layer by lines of stitching. These areas inside the stitching are padded from the back of the work through small slits which are afterwards sewn up.

In Italian (corded) quilting, a design is outlined in parallel lines, and it is then padded by threading between the lines with thick wool.

There is also shadow quilting, in which brightly-coloured fabrics are sandwiched between two layers of transparent fabric so that they show through.

Quilting can be done on a plain ground with a pattern worked in relief; traditionally white or beige plain fabric is used. Wales and County Durham have been particularly associated with this form of quilting, but you can visit museums in many countries to see fine examples of this type of work.

There are three types of quilting suitable for a *patchwork* quilt: "outline" quilting follows the outline of a shape; "in the ditch" quilting follows the seam between the pieces; or you can stitch an alternative pattern on the shape itself.

"Jeremy's Mountain", a quilted wall-hanging by Jenny Bullen.

Traditional quilting

Quilting has always been considered very much a country or "cottage" craft, and was not included among the genteel occupations of the upper and middle classes. So while ladies like Jane Austen might be allowed to do a little patchwork just for amusement, they left quilting to the less well-to-do, for their much-needed bedcovers and warm clothing.

The two areas with the strongest tradition of quilting in the U.K. are Durham and Wales, each of which has its traditional patterns.

Both the photographs on these pages show examples of quilting from South-west Wales, and both were sewn about a hundred years ago. The stitches are quite large and the designs are bold and assured.

The quilts are worked on thick cotton fabric and they are padded either with a blanket or with sheep's wool, probably gathered from the hedgerows. Small tufts of wool are visible in the stitching of the yellow quilt in the picture below.

Popular colours were a soft green (as in the quilt on the left), the bright yellow of the quilt on this page, or sometimes a particularly vivid shade of pink.

The spiral pattern, which is part of a border of the quilt below, is a traditional Welsh quilting design.

Equipment for quilting

Fabric

The most suitable fabric for quilting is pure cotton and this should be smooth, soft and firmly woven. Other suitable fabrics include fabrics made from natural fibres such as silk, fine wool and linen but they must be of a fine, medium-to-lightweight quality. All fabrics to be quilted must be pre-washed to avoid later shrinkage which could easily ruin a carefully quilted bedcover. They must also be tested for colourfastness and if not absolutely fast, discarded. Basically, pure cotton has been and still is the most widely used fabric for quilting as it alone has that obedient floppiness which makes for success, but having emphasized this, many people like to use drip-dry fabrics for washable items. For a bedcover, which should be washable, crease-resistant and also colourfast, cotton/polyester fabrics seem to be a sensible choice for the quilter.

Wadding

This is the middle, padding layer of the quilt and there are several types of wadding you can use.

Synthetic wadding is the most widely used and is very practical. Made from polyester, it is light and springy, easy to sew and it washes very well. It is manufactured in several weights, from 2oz–8oz (60g–240g), 2oz (60g) being the most suitable for bed quilts. The most common width available for polyester wadding is 37in (152cm).

Cotton wadding is made from pure cotton fibres and it needs careful handling and washing. It is a heavier wadding than the synthetic type and well suited for jackets and other garments. It has to be quilted at intervals of not more than about 1½in (4cm), otherwise it forms lumps when it is washed. Dry cleaning is recommended.

Cotton domette is a fabric similar to brushed cotton. It must be pre-shrunk and it provides "body" rather than padding.

Old blankets can also be used for wadding, though they can be rather heavy and a little inflexible for quilting.

Lining

Lining fabric is again best made from pure cotton. Pre-shrunk plain calico or cotton sheeting are both very suitable. The fabric chosen for lining should be firm but at the same time not so closely woven that it is difficult to get your needle through it during quilting.

Needles

"Betweens" are small, fine needles used for quilting. Do not choose too large a needle as it makes unsightly holes in the fabric. Use a new, medium-sized needle for machine-quilting, not a blunt one.

Pins

Pins must be fine and sharp. You can buy extra-long pins that will go through several layers. Glass-headed pins are easier to handle and they will not get lost in the wadding.

Scissors

Three sharp pairs are needed: large for cutting fabric, small for cutting threads and a pair for cutting out paper templates.

Use quilting thread when possible. It is thicker than most threads and is available in all colours. If you cannot obtain it, use cotton-covered polyester or polyester thread, but do not tie-quilt with synthetic thread as the knots will come undone. When quilting patchwork it is impossible to match all the colours, so decide whether you want a sharply contrasting shade or a neutral one, which will blend in.

Thread

Draw polyester and other threads across a piece of beeswax to prevent them knotting. This is not needed for quilting thread.

Beeswax

The receiving finger can soon become sore if not protected during quilting. Use a thimble on the middle finger of your sewing hand if you feel at ease with it. A finger cut from a discarded soft leather glove will protect the underneath finger and many quilters prefer to use this rather than a thimble as it gives more flexibility and contact.

Thimble

A dressmaker's chalk pencil can be used for marking out designs. A pastel pencil, available from artists' suppliers is also recommended and it gives a fine line. Both these can be rubbed off or will rub off by themselves as you go along. Lines can also be outlined with the tip of a needle, which works well on fabrics such as linen, though the mark made does not last long.

Chalk pencil

Washable felt-tipped pens can also be used for marking out designs. Make sure that they *are* washable and that the tip is a fine one. Use only a light pressure.

Washable felt-tipped pen

These can also be used for marking out designs. The pencil should be hard enough to trace sharply, such as HB, but not soft enough to smudge, so avoid B and 2B pencils. Keep points sharp and do not press too hard, then the marks will wear off. A good tip is to use a coloured pencil which is slightly darker in tone but the same colour as the fabric.

Lead pencil

When marking out designs, choose a colour that contrasts with your fabric, i.e. dark for light fabrics, light for dark fabrics. Make sure the carbon paper is not indelible. It can be smudgy.

Dressmaker's carbon paper

Lightweight cardboard is needed for making templates and cereal box cardboard is the ideal thickness.

Cardboard

This is useful for marking straight lines.

Long ruler or yardstick

For cutting out cardboard templates.

Ruler and craft knife

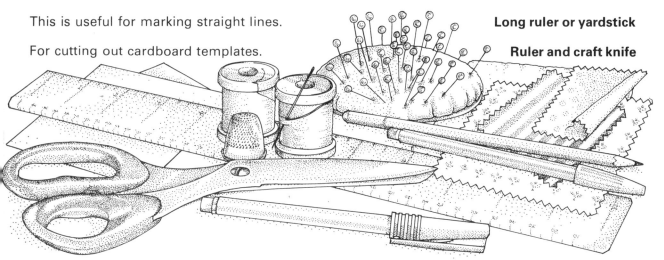

Quilting frames

Many people prefer to quilt without a frame, a method which works very well as long as the three layers are tacked together properly (see opposite) but a quilting frame keeps the work firm and supported.

If working without a frame, roll up the surplus quilt and secure it with large safety pins. Work at a table or sitting cross-legged on a bed, not with the quilt falling onto the floor, as this will move the layers.

Hoop

A hoop, as used for embroidery, may suit your needs. It can be used both for quilting small areas and on large quilts, working on a small area at a time then moving the frame to another part of the quilt. Start at the centre of the quilt and quilt towards the edges. At the edges and corners, extra fabric has to be tacked on so that the hoop can be used there. Wrap strips of muslin around the outer ring of a hoop to protect the work. Do not leave work in a hoop when you are not quilting – it will distort it.

Large frame

If you are making a group quilt, you may wish to quilt it on a large frame, all in one piece.

A large quilting frame consists of two long bars of wood (rollers) with webbing or wide tape tacked to the inner edge on which the fabric is pinned or tacked. There are also two shorter pieces (stretchers) with holes in them for wing nuts or pegs. Rollers are fastened on the stretchers and the quilt is attached to the webbing of one roller, from which it is gradually rolled off onto the other. The quilt is fastened to the stretchers by pinning it to the tapes which keep it firm, but not taut, and these tapes must be re-set after each winding-on.

Large frames rest on a trestle or on the backs of four chairs.

Small frame

A small frame is a scaled-down version of a large one and is suitable for use in most small homes. It can be supported against a table to leave both hands free for quilting.

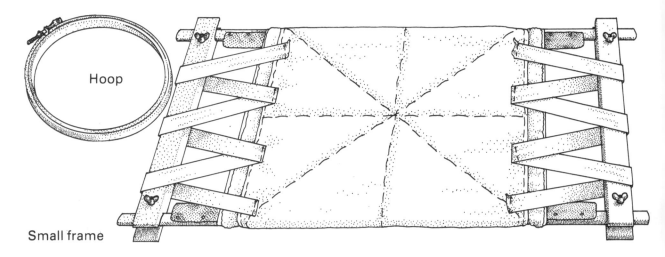

Hoop

Small frame

Before starting

Whether you are working on a frame, quilting without a frame or machine-quilting, the fabric must always be well prepared beforehand so that the three layers are securely held together and do not slip during quilting. To do this, you have to tack the layers together. Use fine stitching and make the stitches firm without pulling too tightly. Work from the centre outwards.

Though preparation may seem very time-consuming, it is an essential part of quilting and the time spent on it is never wasted.

1 Iron the quilt top and mark the quilting lines on the right side of the top layer of the quilt. (See page 60 for transferring patterns.)

2 Ensure that the lining, wadding and top are all crease-free. Iron the lining if it is not, and smooth the wadding.

3 Lay the lining fabric out flat, wrong side up, on a large flat surface such as a clean floor or an old table. Tape the fabric to the surface with masking tape so that it will not move. Pat from the centre outwards so that the fabric is absolutely flat. Avoid pulling.

4 Lay the wadding on top, making sure that it, too, is flat.

5 Lay the quilt top, right side up on top of the wadding. Pat it smooth from the centre without moving the bottom layers.

6 Pin the three layers together, starting at the centre and gently patting outwards as you go. Thoroughly pin all over.

7 Tack the layers together, working from the centre outwards. Tacking is quite difficult to do when the bottom layer is taped to the table and two more layers are pinned to that, but it is necessary to prevent the layers shifting. The distance between two rows of tacking should not be more than 2in (5cm). Tack all around the edges. The more tacking you do the better, whether working with or without a frame or with a hoop.

8 Leave all tacking stitches in until the last quilted stitch is completed. Once the quilting is finished, remove pins and tape.

Setting up work on a quilting frame

1 Prepare the quilt on a large surface, pinning and tacking as described above.

2 Support the frame on chairs of equal height and place a dust sheet on the floor to keep the overhanging fabric clean.

3 Pin one end of the prepared quilt to the webbing of one roller, matching and pinning the centre points of the webbing and quilt edge together, then pinning outwards in opposite directions.

4 Tack the quilt end to the webbing and remove the pins.

5 Wind the quilt onto the roller to which it is already tacked, keeping the tension even.

6 Tack the other end of the quilt to the webbing on the other roller.

7 Adjust wing nuts (or pegs) and rollers for even tension. The work should be firm but not too taut – too much tension makes it too stiff to stitch well.

8 To stretch the sides of the work, place pins through it at approximately 5in (10cm) intervals, about 1in (2.5cm) inside the edge of the quilt. Pin one end of a long piece of tape to a corner of the quilt and wind it around stretchers and pins alternately, in a spiral. Do this along both edges of the quilt.

Designing for quilting

You must plan a quilting design to fit the quilt before you start stitching, to make sure central motifs are central, that border patterns turn corners and that the pattern suits the quilt.

Use the templates given on the following pages or look around you for inspiration for shapes. Lettering, if traced and enlarged, can provide a motif, or you can draw around egg cups, glasses and plates, trace off an eye-catching wallpaper design or make patterns in cut, folded paper. Wrought iron, jewellery and plant forms lend themselves to the flowing lines of quilting.

An attractive pattern can be made by linking, repeating or overlapping a simple motif or reversing it so that it is next to its mirror image. Adapt geometric patchwork shapes or borrow the traditional arrangement of a central design in a square. Do not use small or intricate shapes, as quilting does not lend itself to over-fussy designs. The most effective patterns consist of fairly bold shapes, beautifully arranged and executed.

Make plenty of sketches and draw the chosen design on graph paper. Then make your templates by tracing the design and sticking the tracing onto light cardboard, with paper glue. When dry, cut around the shape with a sharp craft knife. For accuracy, draw shapes such as squares and triangles on graph paper. Stick this to cardboard and cut out as before.

Enlarging a template from 1in to 2in (2.5cm to 5cm)

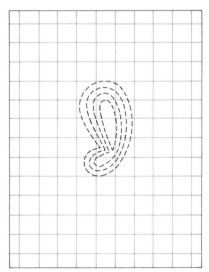  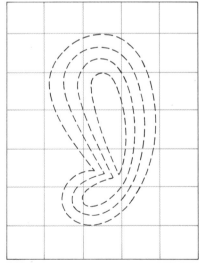

1 Trace the template onto graph (or squared) paper. Measure the height, e.g. 1in (2.5cm). Decide on the finished size, e.g. 2in (5cm).

2 2in (5cm) is twice 1in (2.5cm), so draw the squares on a second piece of paper double the size of those in the first, so that ¼in becomes ½in (and 5mm becomes 1cm).

3 Looking at the first template, copy it onto the larger squares square by square. Take care to make each part of the new drawing match that in the first.

Further examples

If the template size is 1½in (3.5cm) and the required size is 3in (7.5cm), double the size of the squares. If the template size is 1½in (3.5cm) and the required size is 4in (10cm) simplify by adjusting to the nearest multiple of 1½in (3.5cm), in this case 4½in (10.5cm). The squares in the second drawing will be three times larger. To reduce the size of a template, reduce the size of the square proportionately.

Enlarging by projector

Many people take colour slides of subjects such as buildings, wrought ironwork, a design seen over a doorway, or other visual ideas, and slides of suitable designs for quilting can also be purchased in museums. With a projector, paper, pencil and ruler you can turn these designs into templates the correct size for your purposes.

Project the slides onto a wall on which you have taped a large sheet of white paper. By varying the distance between projector and wall the image can be as large or as small as you wish, so adjust the distance between projector and image until your chosen shape is the height you want. Check dimensions with a ruler and draw around the shape on the paper.

Below and on the next few pages are quilting designs, shown in a size that will suit many projects. They can be traced and made into cardboard templates or be enlarged if necessary.

Goose tail or paisley pear

Circle

Cable (can also be used as a border)

Fan

Leaf

*Feather hammock
(can also be used
as a border)*

Small feather

Butterfly

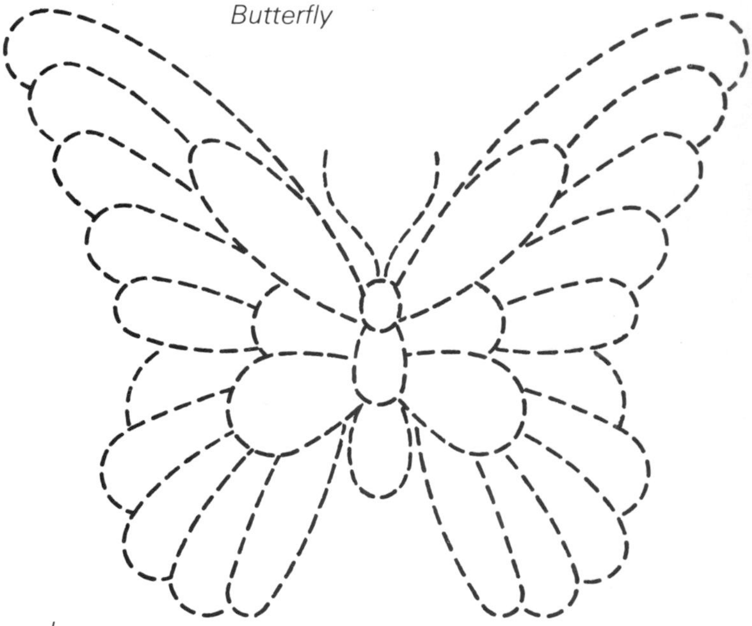

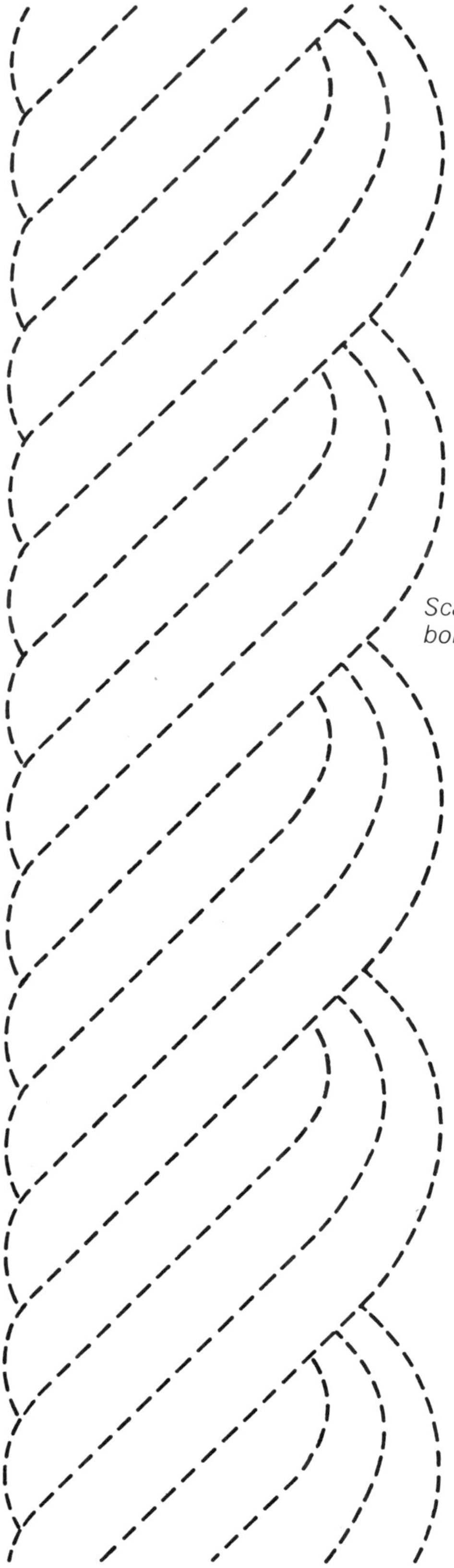

Scalloped border

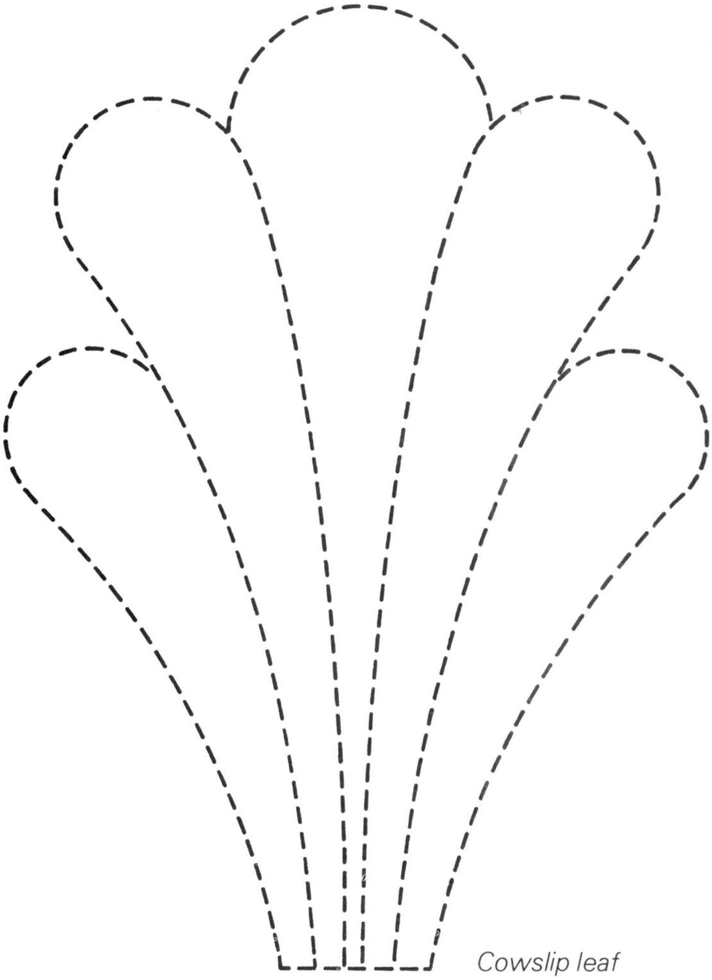

Cowslip leaf

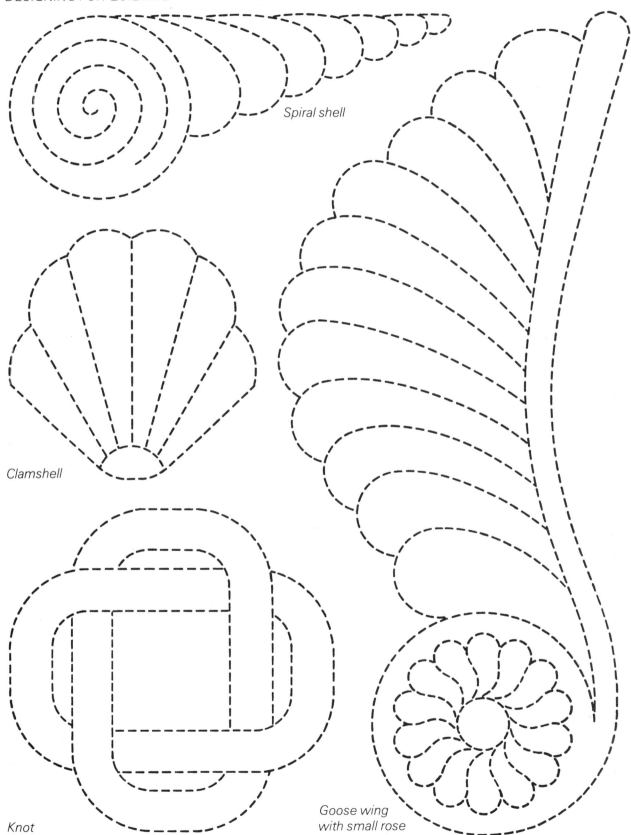

Spiral shell

Clamshell

Knot

Goose wing with small rose

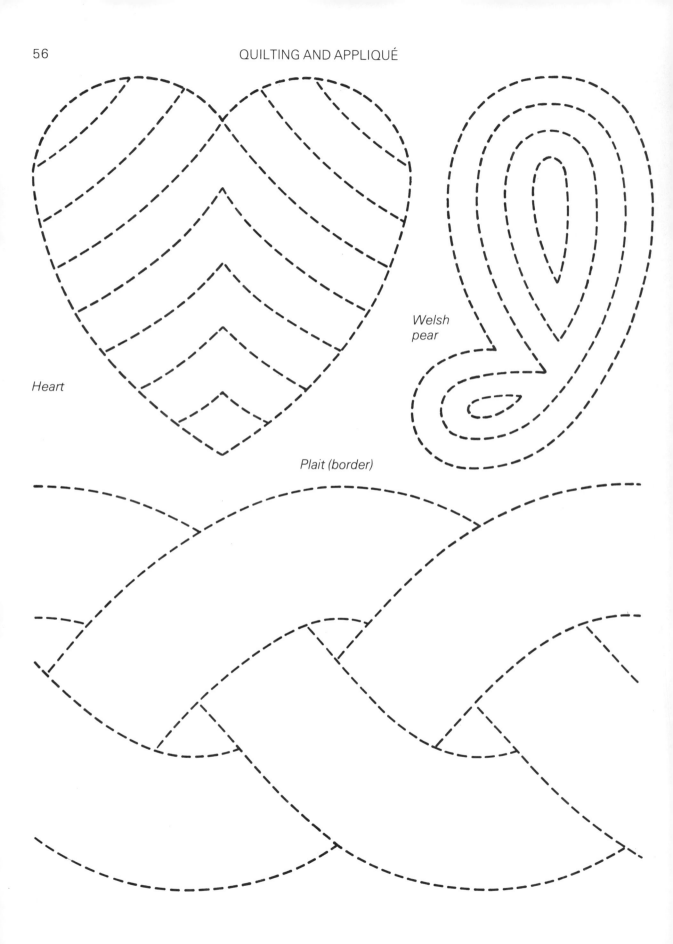

Heart

Welsh
pear

Plait (border)

Rose

Cord and tassel

Leaf

Clam and
feather

Baden
Powell

Heart

Completing the design

Borders

Having chosen your central designs, you should think about borders and "filler" designs and then transfer all these patterns onto the quilt top.

The same quilting techniques apply to border patterns as to any other quilting, except that as there is no central point to them the shapes must be arranged in straight lines. Bear in mind the size of the border, which must balance the central motif, the need for a resting area between centre and border, and fitting the border around corners.

Filler designs

When cotton wadding was widely used, it would form lumps when washed unless it was quilted at least every 2in (5cm), and this led to the creation of various filler designs; but since the advent of synthetic wadding, it is no longer strictly necessary to quilt the entire background surface of a bedcover, though it certainly adds great charm and richness to a quilt.

Filler designs are usually kept very simple so that they do not detract from the more elaborate central and border motifs.

How to transfer patterns

Once you have arrived at a suitable design it must be transferred onto the quilt top and this has to be done before the wadding and backing are attached, otherwise it would be very difficult to transfer the pattern clearly and accurately.

Iron the quilt top and lay it right side up, on a smooth, hard surface. There are several ways of transferring patterns, so choose the one that suits your project best.

On fine, light fabrics, place the template on a piece of white paper larger than the fabric to be quilted and draw around it with a black felt-tipped pen. Carefully centre your drawing under the quilt top, taping it to the fabric with masking tape to prevent it moving and trace the design onto the fabric with coloured pencil or an HB pencil. The pencil marks should last long enough to do the quilting but will have largely disappeared by the finish.

For darker fabrics proceed as above until you reach the tracing stage. Then, back-lighting will be needed to show up the template design. One solution to this is to tape the drawing and fabric to a window so that the design shows through, which will enable you to trace it onto the fabric.

You can also make a light-box. A glass-topped coffee table with a light beneath it makes an excellent light-box, or you can support a thick sheet of glass firmly on two uprights with a light underneath, but do make sure that the glass is supported firmly.

Dressmakers' carbon paper can be used to transfer designs to fabric. Choose a dark colour for light fabrics and a light colour to contrast with dark fabrics. Lay the carbon paper, carbon side down, over the fabric and place the quilt design on top. Trace the design onto the fabric, preferably with a tracing wheel, which will leave a clear but not over-distinct dotted line.

Three different background designs.

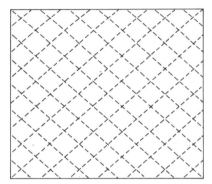

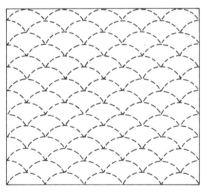

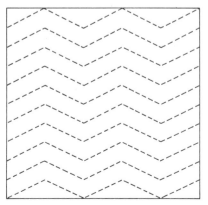

"Quilting" by Jean Gage A.R.C.A.

Hand and machine quilting

Use masking tape to get a straight guideline on fabric for quilting. Peel off after quilting. You can also use the tape to make curves if you clip into it at intervals.

Having completed the design and transferred it to the surface of the fabric, you can begin to quilt either by hand or machine.

Hand-quilting

Start sewing in the centre of the work and quilt outwards. The quilting stitch itself is a small, evenly-spaced running stitch, and there should be approximately five to seven stitches to the inch (2.5cm). It is more important for the stitches to be even than it is for them to be small, though if the stitches are too far apart, the subtleties of the design will be lost. The back of the work should look the same as the top.

Begin by inserting the needle into the wadding along the quilting line and bring it out at the start, leaving a short tail of thread. Take a small backstitch through the top and wadding only, then pierce this backstitch with the needle when taking the first quilting stitch. Continue quilting and once past the tail of the thread, run it off into the wadding.

To fasten off, bring up the thread a little way from the finishing point and work a small backstitch through the wadding and the top. Pierce this backstitch with the needle and run the thread off into the wadding.

With practice you can take more than one stitch at a time and develop rhythmical, even sewing. Thread several needles at a time so that the quilting rhythm is not disturbed by re-threading.

Keep one hand, suitably protected, under the work to feel the needle coming down and to help it back up again.

Use a single strand of thread, as double strands will rub against each other, making them weaker, not stronger. Use short threads. They will neither wear nor twist as much as long ones.

Machine-quilting

Machine-quilting along seams or quilting ⅛in (3mm) parallel to the seams gives a pleasant finish to most work. Designs can also be quilted on a plain ground but take care that the machine does not run away with you and spoil the design, for unpicked mistakes will leave holes.

The work to be machine-quilted must be well tacked otherwise the layers will move as they go through the machine.

Hold the work as flat as possible on either side of the machine foot, allowing the seam to be clearly visible. Stitch along, allowing the stitches to sink down into the groove. It takes practice to ensure that the line of stitching stays exactly on the seam line.

A twin needle not only quilts along the seam but also makes an additional, parallel line of stitching.

When machine-quilting a large quilt, it is very difficult and sometimes impossible to get the bulk through the machine. When that happens, divide the quilt into manageable sections of not more than 36in x 48in (100cm x 120cm). Quilt the sections, join them by hand and cover the raw edges at the back with binding. Or, roll up the quilt, support it on a separate table and feed it through the machine bit by bit.

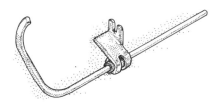

A quilt attachment with an adjustable arm, available for most sewing machines, will make parallel lines when quilting next to or at a distance from a seam. It saves having to mark out parallel lines, as it regulates them automatically.

Knotting or tying

First pin, then tack the three layers. Using linen thread or crochet cotton and working from the centre outwards, either tie the knots on the patchwork seams or make them part of the design and tie them, front or back.

A quilted cot cover made by members of Tadworth WI, Surrey.

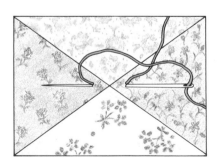

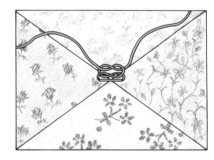

1 Make a ¼ in (6mm) stitch through all thicknesses and make a backstitch, leaving a 3in (7.5cm) tail.

2 Pull the thread through, then cut the thread, leaving another 3in (7.5cm) tail.

3 Tie ends in a reef knot, pull tight and cut thread ends about 1¼ in (3cm) from the knot.

The story of appliqué

Appliqué is a French word meaning "applied", and it is used to describe the sewing of small cut-out pieces of fabric onto a larger background piece. The edges of the small pieces are carefully turned under and hemmed and then applied or layered to the larger piece. Appliquéd tops are used for quilt-making in the same way as pieced tops.

This form of quilt-making was popular in America at the same time as patchwork, that is from about 1775 to 1875. Although the idea of cutting out designs and motifs from fabric and sewing them onto another may seem laborious, it must be remembered that at one time printed cottons were rare and expensive. Many of the early appliqué quilts were made from imported chintz which had quickly become very fashionable and highly sought after; the precious fabric went further when it was cut up and used in this way, which is known as appliqué *perse*.

Many forms of appliqué quilt developed at this time, among them the wedding quilt, which was given to the bride by her friends; the album quilt, in which each block was made by a different person and signed; and the "freedom quilt" given to a young man on his twenty-first birthday. (Until his majority, a young man was the property of his parents and could be apprenticed without his consent.) There were also "medallion quilts" in which a central medallion was surrounded by a series of borders. A typical design of this type might be a central basket or garland of flowers surrounded by borders of flowers, often in baskets.

The general effect of all these appliquéd quilts was one of great warmth and richness. Colours were usually predominantly reds, oranges and browns on a white ground and the finished quilts were beautifully made.

Close-up photographs of two of the motifs on the quilt opposite.

Appliqué and patchwork quilt made by Copthorne WI, Surrey.

Designing for appliqué

Designing for appliqué is much like designing for block patterns. Draw a few designs to fit on a block on graph paper and colour them in different ways. As in designing a pieced block, when designing an asymmetrical appliqué block, place four copies of the pattern together to reach the total effect, or use the hand-mirror method described previously.

Appliqué enables you to increase the curved shapes in a quilt design. Use them on their own or with geometric shapes.

Other ways of designing for appliqué are to use the folded paper method, cutting into a folded square and opening it out to discover the pattern made. Or trace shapes from books, working out designs on squared paper in order to see where to plan the spaces, which are just as important as the shapes.

Remember that a design need not be all in one piece. Some of it can be in the form of islands, standing among the main shapes.

Draw a line to show the hem allowance all the way around each shape you design, ¼in (6mm) outside the sewing line.

Whichever method you use, make sure that none of the shapes or parts of the shapes are very narrow. They should never be less than ½in (1.25cm) wide: raw edges are difficult to hem.

"Bridge" appliqué cushion by Janet Wolchover.

Applying the shapes

The equipment needed for appliqué is the same as that used for patchwork and quilting: needle and thread, scissors, thimble and colourfast, unshrinkable fabrics.

Lightweight cottons are the most suitable for use in appliqué. Heavy fabrics are difficult to hem neatly and their bulk prevents a good, flat finish. Fabrics that fray are difficult, too.

As the appliqué motifs are cut from prepared templates, you will also need tracing paper and pencil to trace out your shapes, and thin cardboard for templates.

The outline of the templates is the sewing line and unlike patchwork, the design is drawn on the right side of the fabric, so that you can see where to fold under the shapes to hem them. Use sharp, hard pencils to mark the outline, light on dark fabrics, dark on light.

Allow the usual ¼in (6mm) for a seam all around the shapes. Use lightweight, iron-on bonding to strengthen and reinforce the appliqué shapes if you want them really smooth, cutting it to the sewing line.

If using a sewing machine, follow the same method as for hand stitching (below), then machine stitch on the right side with small, straight, zigzag or satin stitches. With satin stitch, there is no need to hem the shapes before stitching, as the close stitches cover the raw edges.

Not all edges have to be hemmed. Sometimes, the raw edges of one appliqué piece will slip under the hemmed edges of a neighbouring piece.

On very small shapes, starch can be applied with a small paint brush. This will give a firm outline even to polyester cottons, which on the whole do not fold well. Be careful when pressing hems not to get marks on the right side. Leave the templates in, tack in place and then iron on the wrong side of the fabric.

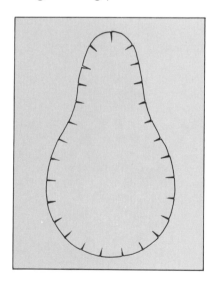

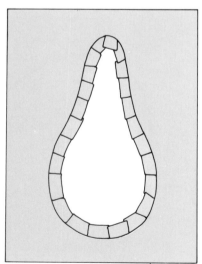

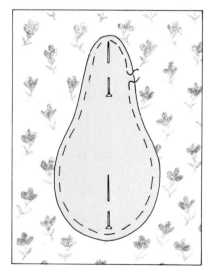

1 Clip into the seam allowance almost up to the sewing line on all curved shapes so that they will turn under satisfactorily.

2 With the template in position, turn the seam allowance under and iron flat. Remove the template after ironing.

3 Pin and tack the motif onto the background and stitch with small stitches. If you want the stitches to show, use buttonhole, cross or feather stitch.

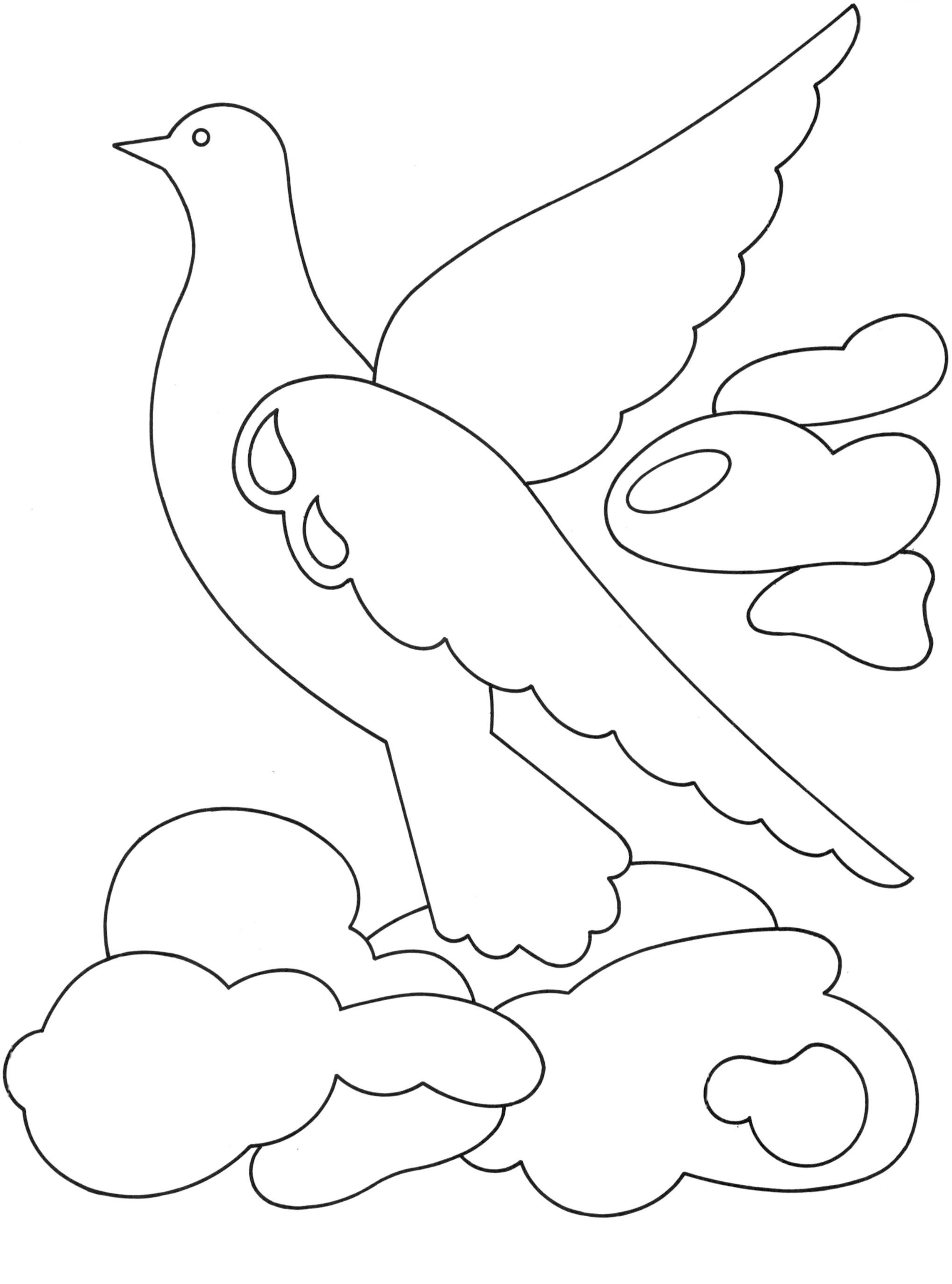

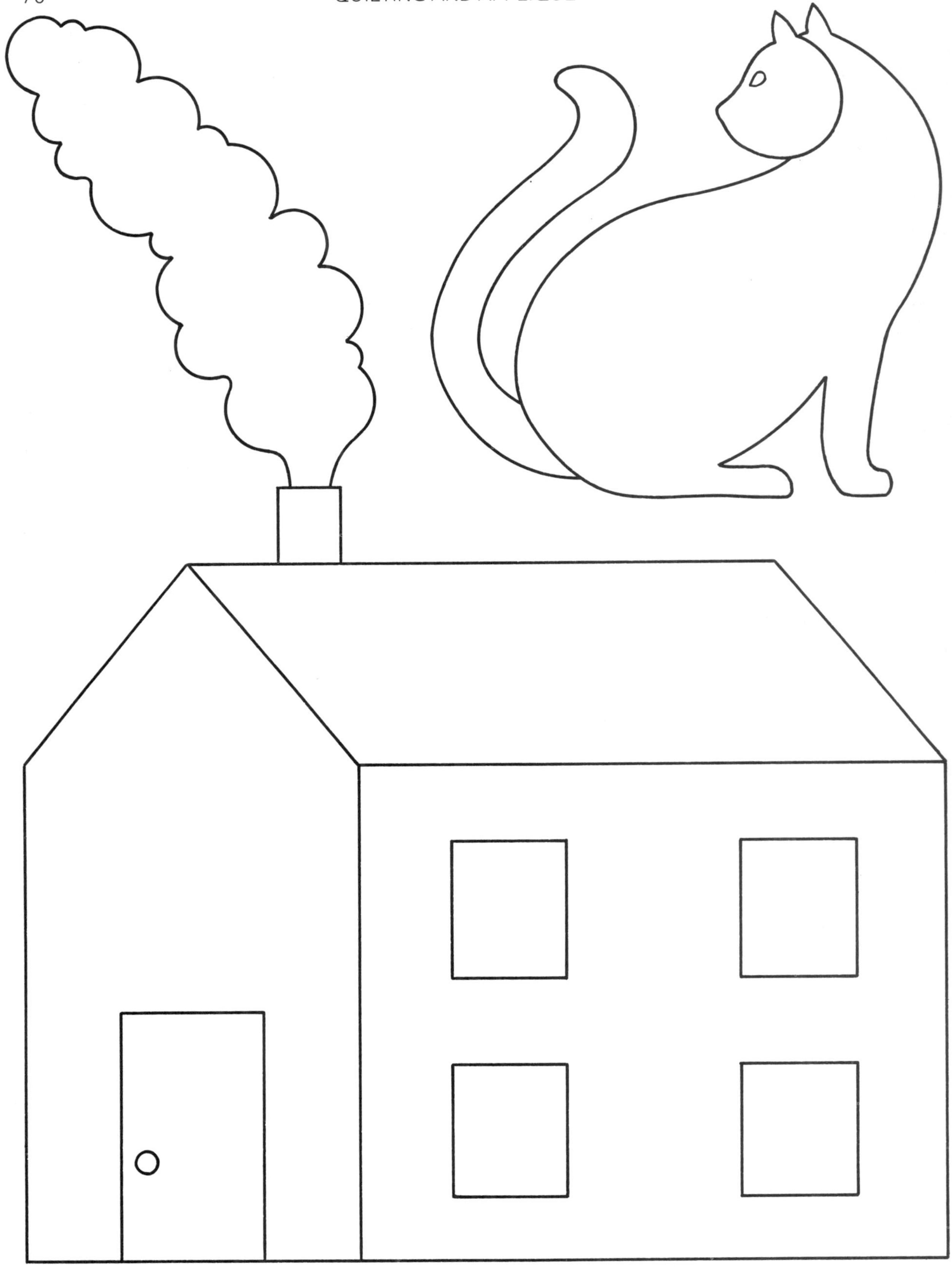

MAKING A QUILT

A quilt is one of the most satisfying of all things to make in patchwork. The endless permutations of shape and colour offer scope for artistic skill as well as a challenge for those who enjoy producing something useful and decorative.

There are a great many styles to choose from. A strip quilt with its parallel bands of colour can be uncomplicated yet effective; an all-over pattern in one shape (such as a hexagon) is a traditionally English style, while block quilts or appliqué designs surrounded by borders are always pleasing. Adventurous quilters are breaking away from these well-loved styles altogether and making quilts which look like fine abstract paintings.

Estimating quantities

Always avoid using the selvedges of the fabric even though it may seem convenient at the time. They may shrink when washed later on.

First consider the size of the quilt you wish to make. This can vary from cot to full bed size. Measure the bed, allowing for an 18in (46cm) overhang if you want one, at the sides and bottom and about 20in (50cm) extra to cover the pillows. You may prefer a frill to an overhang, in which case the pattern should fit the bed top.

For a block quilt, the size of the block is critical in the planning stages. Blocks can be any size you like, but usually they vary from about 10in (25cm) to 16in (41cm) square. Each block should fit on top of or down the sides of the bed, not hang half-way over the sides. Make a drawing on graph paper showing the size of the bed and the overhangs and calculate how many blocks are needed and how big they should be.

The size of the blocks will also depend on the width of the lattices and borders, so these should be decided at this stage too. Lattices can be any size but usually they are from 2in (5cm) to 4in (10cm) wide. All measurements can be adjusted to fit the size of the bed.

Long strips should be cut on the length of the fabric to avoid having to piece them and all strips must be on the straight of the fabric. If possible, cut all strips so that they will lie in the same direction on the finished quilt, as the colour of a fabric may change depending on which direction it is placed.

Always include seam allowances when estimating quantities and in addition about 6in (15cm) extra fabric all around in the sum total, which will be accounted for by quilting loss.

Adjust odd half inches up rather than down; allow for more fabric rather than less. When using window templates, allow even more fabric to enable you to pick out particular patterns.

Measure odd scraps of fabric by ironing them, then laying them out on the table to the required width, then proceeding as below. Subtract the amount of fabric you may already have by you in scraps from the total you plan to buy.

Dressmaking fabrics are usually sold in 36in, 44/45in or sometimes 54/60in (90cm, 112/115cm and 140/150cm) widths. Curtain fabrics are usually sold in 48in and 54in (122cm and 140cm) widths and sheeting in 90in (228cm) widths. It is also possible to buy white pure cotton in 105in (280cm) widths in some shops.

To estimate how much of each colour you need for a block pattern, work from your sketch plan, taking one shape in one colour at a time.

1 Calculate how many times this shape appears in one block.
2 Multiply this number by the number of blocks you need to make the whole patchwork.
3 Lay the template for the chosen shape on a standard width (say 36in (90cm) or 48in (120cm)) of fabric and work out how many times it will fit into that width.
4 Divide the number of shapes needed for the whole patchwork by the number of shapes you can fit in a row.
5 Multiply this number by the height of the shapes. This will give you the amount of fabric needed for this particular shape and colour. Repeat for other shapes and colours.

A quilt by a group from Port Townsend, Washington, U.S. (By courtesy of Marjorie Abraham).

Finishing touches

Joining block patterns with lattices
When the blocks are complete, they must be pieced together so that their patterns match precisely. If using lattices, measure and cut the short lattices to go between the blocks first, to the width calculated plus ½in (1.25cm) at each long edge and at the ends to allow for seams.

Pin and sew a complete vertical row of blocks and short lattices plus seam allowance and press on the wrong side towards the darkest fabrics. Then pin and sew the vertical rows of blocks to long lattices and press as before.

Cut the two end and two side strips for the border, each plus ½in (1.25cm) seam allowance along one side and ends, plus an extra inch (2.5cm) along the outside edge for finishing. Pin and sew on border strips.

Joining wadding
To avoid forming ridges when joining wadding strips together, butt the pieces together and stitch them with ladder or herringbone stitch so that the edges will not overlap. When sewing thick wadding pieces together, "step" the join, also to avoid ridges.

Linings
Linings neaten the back of a quilt and strengthen it. They should be lightweight and cut on the straight of the fabric. They should also be attached to the quilt top and to the wadding, to prevent them ballooning out and sagging. Quilting does this automatically but other methods of attaching the layers are embroidery, placed at intervals or all over the quilt, and tying (described on page 63).

The width of the fabric obtainable may not be wide enough for a large quilt and it may be necessary to join the lining. To avoid placing unwanted strain on the centre seam, cut one length of the lining in half lengthways and stitch a half width to each long side

Binding corners

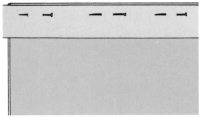

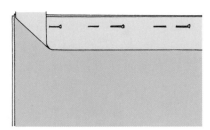

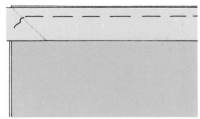

1 Use straight, not bias, binding. Trim all the quilt edges and pin the right side of the binding to the right side of the work through all layers. Pin to the first corner.

2 Mitre the corner by folding the binding to make a 90° angle. Pinch along the fold to make a definite crease-line.

3 Tack and then machine-stitch the binding through all layers up to the inner corner of the crease. Fasten off the threads.

of the full width. Allow extra fabric all around if you intend to bring the lining to the front and use it for binding.

Quilting edges

A quilting edge is the easiest method of finishing a quilt. Trim the edges of lining and top and turn them in. Trim wadding edges close to the sewing line. Tack and then join top and lining with a single or a double row of evenly-sewn running stitches.

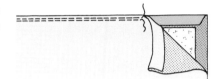

Binding with the lining or the top

If you plan ahead you can cut the lining or top fabric large enough to make the binding. Allow at least 1½in (4cm) more than the top or the lining. Trim all around, turn in the raw edges, press, then fold the lining or top over the edges. Pin, tack and hem or machine in place.

Strip binding

This type of binding is sewn on after attaching the lining. It must be cut on the bias for curves but straight binding can be used for straight edges. Join bias strips with diagonal seams.

Piped edges

Piping gives a firm, neat edge and protects the quilt from wear. Shrink piping cord before use, knotting the ends: boil it and let it drip dry. Apply piping before attaching the lining. Allow about 6in (15cm) more than the finished required length.

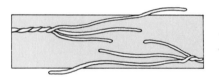

To pipe, cut a bias strip about 1¼in (3.5cm) wide and as long as the cord. Lay the cord down the middle of the strip on the reverse side, fold it over and stitch close to the cord. Place the prepared piping cord along the edge of the quilt, between lining and top, both of which have their edges turned in. Sew just below the seam line.

For a neat finish, try to prevent piping joins coming at the join of two or more patches and always splice piping cord to join it.

To splice, overlap the cord ends by 1in (2.5cm) and separate the three plies of cord. Leave one uncut, cut back the second ply by ½in (1.25cm) and the third by 1in (2.5cm). Twist the two ends of the cord together and bind them firmly with thread.

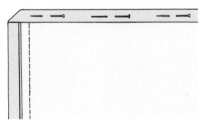

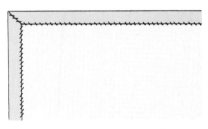

4 Fold the mitred corner up along its crease and down again along the next edge. Pin, tack and stitch the second edge from the corner of the crease. Do all four edges like this and join the two ends of the binding with a diagonal seam where they meet.

5 Turn the work to the wrong side and fold the binding so that it meets the line of machine stitching. Pin in place.

6 Pin and fold the corners into neat mitres and hem the edges of the binding and of the corner seams in place.

Making a wall-hanging

Group quilts are often put on display and some people feel that a quilt is best appreciated when it is hung on a wall, like a picture. Below are three ways of adapting a quilt into a wall-hanging.

Visible loops
Before adding the lining, fold in half and sew 3in (8cm) squares of lining fabric along one edge and one end to make small tubes. Turn the tubes right side out, turn in the raw edges and stitch closed. Press.

Fold each tube in half and tack the two free ends to the top edge of the right side of the quilt at measured intervals, with the tops of the loops facing towards the centre of the quilt.

With right sides together, tack and sew the lining in place, sewing over the loops and leaving 12in (30cm) unstitched along one side. Turn right side out, stitch the gap, quilt or tie. Slide a rod through the loops.

Sleeve
Cut a 5in (12cm) wide piece of lining fabric to the width of the quilt. Fold it in half lengthwise with right sides together and seam along one edge and down one end.

Turn right side out, turn the raw edges in, and stitch closed. Press. Sew this strip to the back of the top of the quilt, hemming top and bottom to form a tube. This will hold a rod which can be suspended at each end by cords.

Invisible loops
Use either of the above methods to stitch small loops or a sleeve at the back of the quilt instead of at the top, to hold a rod.

"Papaver", a wall-hanging by Isabel Dibden.

Caring for your quilt

Storage

There are three ways of storing a quilt: flat, folded or rolled. Since few people have the space to store quilts flat, a compromise is to keep them on a bed or hang them on the wall. This way they will be kept flat and aired as well as appreciated. However, if there really is no space to display them, they must be put away, and then they should be either folded or rolled.

The disadvantage of rolling is that a prolonged period of such treatment will affect the fabric and evenness of the wadding, but the method can work if the folds are changed at regular intervals. The best way of folding is to gently fanfold (concertina) the quilt with the minimum of folds, at the same time laying crumpled tissue or tissue and wrapping paper tubes in the folds to ease the stress on the fabric. Do not stack more than two quilts on top of each other as their weight will crush the quilts beneath. Lay them on a cotton sheet on a shelf and bring the sheet up around the quilts in a parcel, so that they are kept free of dust during storage.

Rolling is another good method of storage and one that is used in the textile departments of many museums. Here the quilts are rolled around furnishing fabric rollers, which can be obtained from many furnishing stores, then placed in a long cotton bag which is especially made to fit loosely over the roller. A draw-string top allows air to circulate a little and at the same time keeps the dust out. It is a good idea when using either of these storage methods to get the quilts out every now and then and give them a good shake and an airing.

Never store quilts in plastic, as this prevents the air circulating, which could cause a musty smell or, if there is any dampness, mould.

Cleaning

Quilts laid out on a bed or hung on the wall gather dust, which dulls the colours and can be corrosive. Dust must be gently removed with a vacuum cleaner. When using a vacuum cleaner, stretch a piece of muslin across the suction end of the cleaner and secure it with an elastic band to avoid damaging fabrics, especially old quilts. Not all quilts can be washed and your quilt is best dry-cleaned if the colours are non-fast or if it contains cotton wadding, which tends to get lumpy if washed. It is inadvisable to wash silk, wool or very old and fragile quilts, nor should you try to wash a quilt so large that it would be unmanageable when wet. If you have to dry-clean, air quilts thoroughly afterwards.

To wash a quilt, fill a bath with warm water in which you have dissolved enough good, non-biological washing powder to make a lather. (Soap flakes are even safer.) Place the unfolded quilt in the water and squeeze the suds through gently with your hands.

To rinse, empty the bath and squeeze out as much water as possible, then refill the bath with warm water and repeat the rinsing until the water is clear. Avoid lifting the quilt unless it is well supported.

If the quilt will fit, a short spin in a washing machine is helpful, but in any case, dry quickly away from direct heat, preferably on a windy day over two parallel clothes lines, face down, if sunny, to prevent fading. Alternatively support the quilt on a frame.

Pad clothes lines, and especially single ones, with strips of old sheeting to prevent marking the quilt while drying.

Making a group quilt:

It is well known that quilting "bees" or parties have a long tradition in America but perhaps less well known that there were similar social gatherings in the U.K. In the North and in Wales, many bedcovers were quilted by church, chapel and Women's Institute sewing groups, a tradition that is being carried on today. Making a quilt is a pleasant occupation for a small group of people who enjoy sewing in company, for when shared among several workers a quilt grows so rapidly that everyone soon has the satisfaction of seeing the results of their creative efforts.

However, a quilt will not organize itself and there must be a leader to coordinate its making — someone to act as king-pin, someone to motivate, advise, check, instruct and, above all, to delegate.

The organizer should have had some experience of quilting but she does not necessarily have to work on the quilt herself, for there will be plenty of other things to occupy her time, such as making sure everyone keeps up with the schedule. Someone has to supervise the planning session, organize the buying of the fabrics, the cutting-out of templates and fabrics, the assembly of kits plus instructions, and the joining and quilting of finished blocks or sections (for not all group quilts are block quilts). The person to do all this is the organizer.

If the quilt is to be raffled for fund-raising, it is a good idea to make a few spare blocks to take around, so that everyone buying a ticket can see what they may win.

1

2

Planning the blocks

3

4

5

Collect all the equipment needed and decide on the size of the quilt and whether you want lattices and a border. Calculate the size and number of blocks from this.

1 Everyone should draw a simple block pattern on graph paper in coloured felt-tipped pens or in crayons. Colour the various parts of the pattern in different tones and colours. (See chapter one for designing blocks.)

2 Choose one pattern and draw it four times to see the overall design it makes when they are fitted together.

3 Decide whether you want the blocks to alternate with blank blocks or with different types of blocks and experiment with various border patterns.

4 Draw as much of the block as you need to actual size on graph paper to show all the shapes needed to make up a block. Outline clearly one of each shape required and cut it out of the graph paper.

5 Make templates by sticking a new piece of graph paper onto thin cardboard, arranging the previously cut shapes on this and drawing around them. Draw in a seam allowance line of ¼ in (6mm) around each shape, and colour this in. Accuracy is very important during all stages.

Making a group quilt:

6

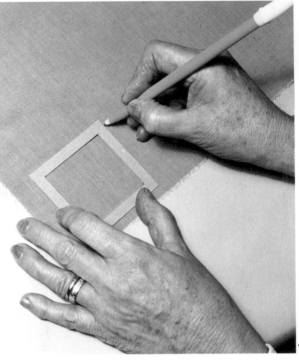

7

8

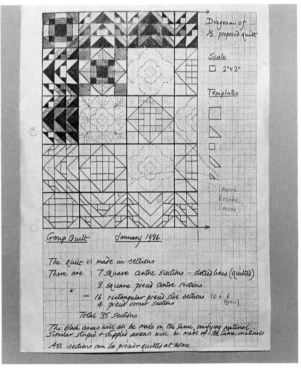

9

Cutting and sewing

10

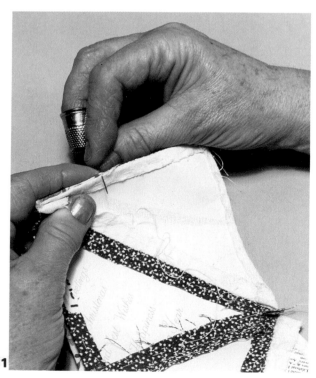

11

Cut around both these pencil lines to make window templates, cutting them out with a sharp craft knife against a steel ruler. Put scraps of sample fabrics on a white sheet on the floor to help everyone decide on a basic colour scheme. A unifying colour and some others will probably have to be purchased – or you can dye fabrics.

6 To find a satisfactory colour scheme, cut sample pieces roughly the size of the templates and arrange them in different colourways in the chosen block pattern on a white background. Cut enough pieces to show several different arrangements of colour. As a rough guide, start with the darkest colour in the centre.

When the colour scheme is decided, count the number of patches needed of each colour in one block and multiply that by the total number of blocks. (See estimating quantities, page 74). Remember to allow for lattices, if any, and borders. Buy necessary fabrics.

Wash all fabrics to test them for colourfastness and possible shrinkage. Discard any not colourfast. Press fabrics well on the wrong side.

7 Place window templates on the wrong side of the fabrics and draw around the outside of the templates with a washable felt-tipped pen or a sharp pencil.

Cut out the fabric shapes with sharp scissors on the outside drawn line.

8 Cut templates out of thick paper (such as Christmas cards) with a sharp craft knife to the inside measurement of the window templates. Assemble all cut fabric shapes into kits, one kit for each block, and pin the arrangement onto a piece of old sheeting or spare fabric a little larger than block size, so that it can be rolled up and taken away by each member of the group. Add paper templates, needles and thread to each kit if necessary.

9 Give everyone a photocopy showing the whole quilt design and include on it information such as the size of the quilt, the border pattern, what needles and thread are required, areas to be quilted, dates of meetings, explanatory notes and initials of who is doing what.

10 Make up the patchwork shapes. Place the paper templates on the reverse side of the fabric, matching the pencil lines. Fold the fabric over the templates. Pin and tack.

11 Oversew on the reverse side when joining patches, with tiny stitches.

Making a group quilt:

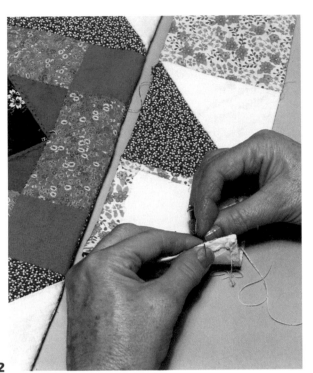

12

13

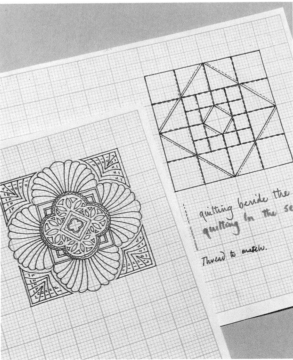

14

15

Joining and finishing

16

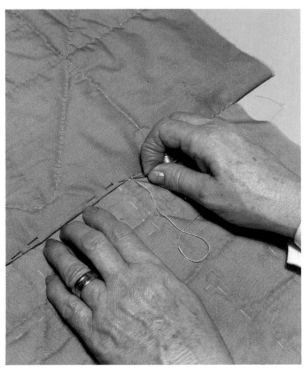

17

12 When making up the blocks, plan the work so that you sew in strips when possible to avoid having to sew into corners, which prevents the work lying flat. If there are lattices, sew them to the blocks in strips too. First add the short lattices, then sew the strips of blocks plus short lattices to the long lattices.

13 Pin the patchwork pieces in place before sewing the blocks together. Ease if necessary to get a perfect pattern match.

14 Decide where each block is to be quilted and give each person a diagram of it on graph paper. Decide whether to quilt in matching or contrasting thread and how many stitches to the inch.

15 When the patchwork is completed, remove the paper templates, leaving seam allowances around the outside turned under to retain the shape of the blocks. Tack.

If the quilting is all in one, join the completed blocks, prepare the frame for quilting and quilt as described on pages 48 and 63.

For individual quilting, press the unquilted blocks. Cut the lining and wadding 1in (2.5cm) larger all around for each block and tack the lining, wadding and top as described on page 49.

Quilt along the block seams or ⅛in (3mm) parallel to the seams.

16 After quilting, trim the wadding of each block to exactly the same size as the pieced top of the block.

Oversew the pieced, quilted tops of adjoining blocks, on the wrong side, in strips.

Join the completed strips of blocks together, oversewing the wrong sides of adjoining strips. Butt-join the wadding with ladder stitch and overlap the linings as shown next.

17 To join the block linings, lay strips of adjoining blocks flat. Trim the underneath lining only to the same size as the top wadding. Pin the linings one over the other, then hem together with the linings overlapping. Work and join the borders as for blocks. Finish the edges in one of the ways shown on pages 76–7.

It is a nice finishing touch to sign and date your quilt using embroidery thread.

A photograph of the completed quilt appears on page 155.

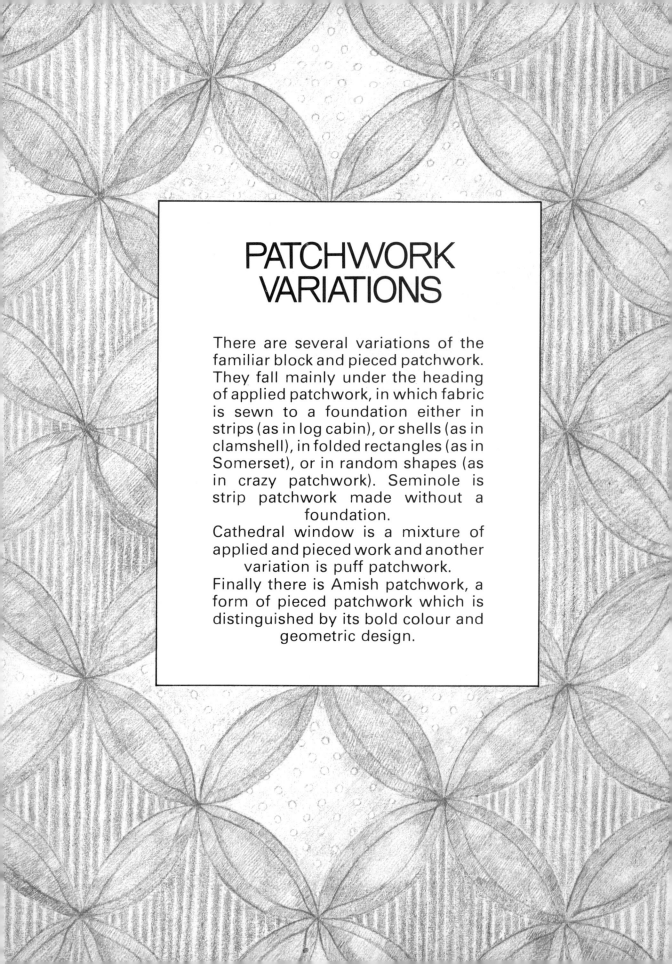

PATCHWORK VARIATIONS

There are several variations of the familiar block and pieced patchwork. They fall mainly under the heading of applied patchwork, in which fabric is sewn to a foundation either in strips (as in log cabin), or shells (as in clamshell), in folded rectangles (as in Somerset), or in random shapes (as in crazy patchwork). Seminole is strip patchwork made without a foundation.

Cathedral window is a mixture of applied and pieced work and another variation is puff patchwork.

Finally there is Amish patchwork, a form of pieced patchwork which is distinguished by its bold colour and geometric design.

Log cabin

Log cabin is an early form of block patchwork. Each block is composed of narrow strips of light and dark overlapping fabrics which may be patterned or plain, built out from a central square, often giving a three-dimensional effect. When the blocks are joined, the positioning of the light "logs" and the dark determines the overall pattern.

The ends of the strips overlap and are supposed to represent the log structures of the cabins of early American settlers. Some of the traditional arrangements of the patterned squares have titles such as "barn raising", "straight furrow" or "goose flight", that echo the early pioneering days of the U.S.

In log cabin patchwork, the stitches are concealed by using reverse sewn turnings, which makes it suitable for machine-work, though it takes practice to machine the strips accurately.

The blocks of patches are usually sewn onto a foundation material, making the finished bedcover durable as well as warm; but if firm, even-weight material is used instead, a quilt can be made without this extra layer.

You cannot buy templates for log cabin patchwork because everything needs its own set of templates for its own block size. Below is shown the method for making a 5¾in (15cm) square.

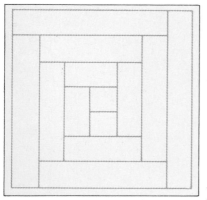 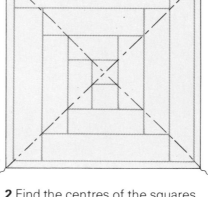 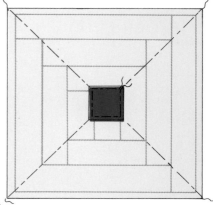

1 Cut a cardboard foundation template that is 5¾in (15cm) square, plus an extra ¼in (5mm) seam allowance all round. Using the outline of the template, cut squares of foundation material out of firm cotton to this size. To ensure accuracy, mark out each fabric square before stitching, with lines showing where the patchwork strips are to go, using graph paper, dressmaker's carbon paper and tracing wheel.

2 Find the centres of the squares by folding them diagonally. Tack along the diagonals so that you can use the tacked lines as guides. With experience you will not need the guides.

3 Make another template 1¼in (3cm) square from fabric that will provide an accent of colour to the finished block. Pin and then tack the centre square to the centre of the foundation patch, lining up corners with the diagonal lines. Raw edges will be covered by succeeding strips. This square will measure approximately ¾in (2cm) when the other strips are sewn to it; i.e. the seam allowance is approximately ¼in (5mm).

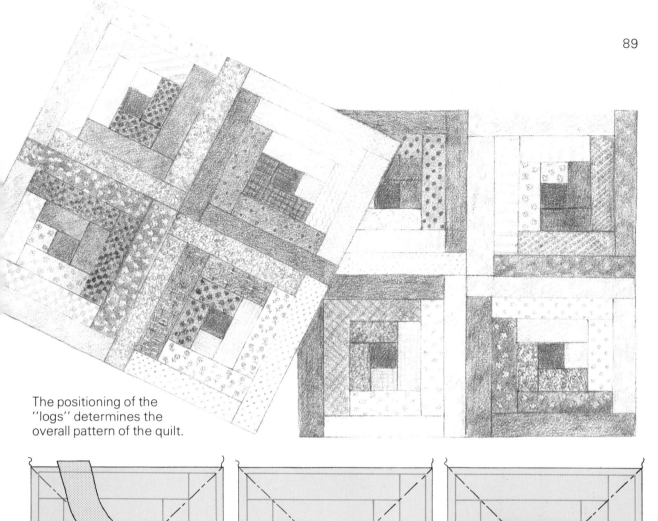

The positioning of the "logs" determines the overall pattern of the quilt.

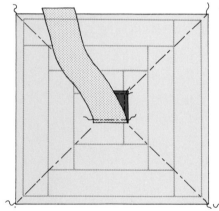

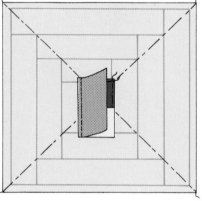

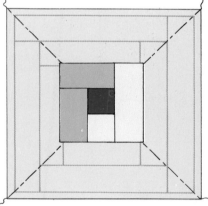

4 Cut a few strips about 1¼ in (3cm) wide on the straight of the material – across the width of the fabric is a good length. Use two tones of one colour: light and dark. Lay the light strip over the centre patch face down, matching the edge with one edge of the square. Tack in place. Cut off excess of strip so that the light strip lines up exactly with the centre square. Stitch ¼ in (5mm) from the edge. Turn over and press flat.

5 Proceeding clockwise (or anti-clockwise if you like, but make sure that all the blocks are sewn in the same direction), take a dark strip and lay it at right angles to the first strip and the centre square. Cut off the excess so that it lines up exactly with the end of the centre square. Stitch down ¼ in (5mm) from the edge. Turn and press flat.

6 Add the third (dark) and fourth (light) strips in the same way, overlapping the ends of the previous strips. Repeat on following rounds. The seam allowance of the first round is covered by the next round. Keep the correct sequence of darks and lights throughout. Fold over the final round of strips so that they meet the edges of the foundation square. Tack all edges together. Join the finished squares, right sides facing.

Log cabin quilt by Upchurch WI, East Kent.

Here are two variations of the log cabin design, in which strips of fabric are placed in different sequences or arrangements of light and dark around a central square. The technique remains unchanged.

Pineapple
In the pineapple pattern, light strips are placed diagonally across the corners of dark strips on alternate rounds.

The block requires a template for the centre square and for each round of progressively longer strips. Complete the blocks with a triangle at each corner.

When the blocks are joined, place the dark fabrics together so that they form an overall design of spikey-edged squares or crosses (as shown below).

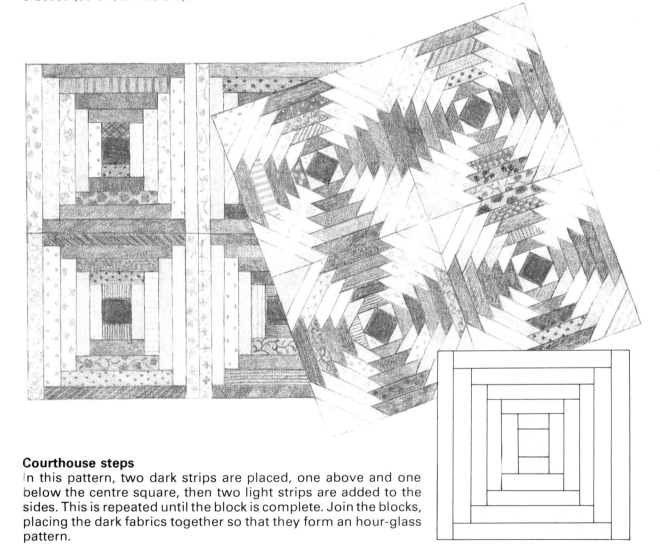

Courthouse steps
In this pattern, two dark strips are placed, one above and one below the centre square, then two light strips are added to the sides. This is repeated until the block is complete. Join the blocks, placing the dark fabrics together so that they form an hour-glass pattern.

Cathedral window

This intricate patchwork is made by joining folded and re-folded foundation squares of fabric and decorating them with applied patches of brightly-coloured fabrics.

A pin cushion made from a single piece of cathedral window patchwork, by Valerie Ibbett.

Making a foundation square by machine-sewing

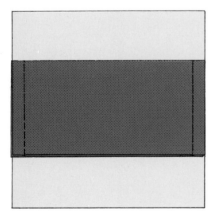

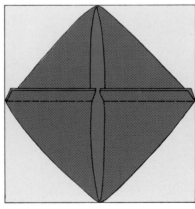

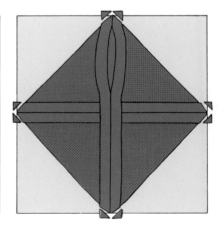

1 Fold squares of fabric in half, right sides together, and machine the two short ends, leaving a ¼ in (6mm) seam allowance.

2 Without turning right side out, hold the centres of the unstitched sides and pull so that the fabric forms a square.

3 Sew the remaining seams together, leaving a gap for turning. Press seams open and clip excess fabric off outside corners. Turn right side out and press. Fold corners of square to centre, pin, secure with a centre stitch as in steps 2 and 3 opposite; continue as in step 4.

The foundation squares can be machine or hand sewn. Use small, fine pins, and use cotton fabric, as it is more difficult to make a crisp fold with synthetics.

To make an accurate foundation square, cover both sides of the template with fine sandpaper and iron the fabric edges over the template. Remove the template and press the edges again.

Cut foundation squares twice as large as are required for the finished square, plus a ¼in (6mm) seam allowance all around. After pinning the foundation squares (step 1 below), you can stitch the four points together, then remove the pins.

Making a hand-sewn foundation square

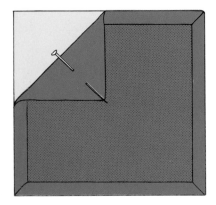

1 Fold a ¼in (6mm) hem all around and press. Fold corners to centre, with wrong sides together and pin.

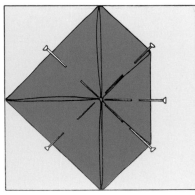

2 Fold corners to centre again and pin. First pins should lie in the gaps between folds.

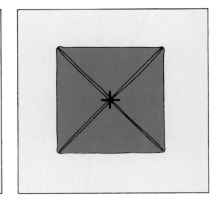

3 Remove first pins and stitch centre firmly with a neat cross, sewing through to the back. Remove second pins.

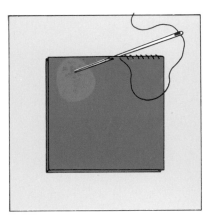

4 Place two completed foundation squares together, folded sides facing, and oversew one edge neatly, corner to corner, in matching thread. Make sure there are no gaps at corners.

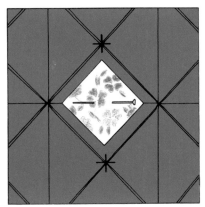

5 Continue to sew foundation squares together until you have enough. Cut coloured squares about ¼in (6mm) smaller all around than the completed foundation squares and arrange them over the seams, with the grain running the same way on each. Pin in place.

6 Curl one edge of the foundation fabric over the edge of a coloured square. Stitch with tiny stitches in matching thread through to the back of the fabric, around each side of the coloured square.

Clamshell

This combines pieced with applied patchwork. The patches are built up in overlapping rows, each row stitched to the one above. A cork board is a help when assembling the patches.

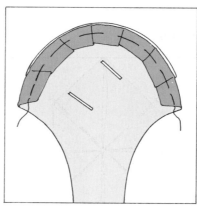

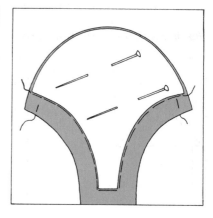

1 Prepare thin cardboard shapes from the template as for hexagons. Cut patches on the straight of the fabric. Pin the template to the right side of the fabric patch with two pins placed diagonally to prevent pulling the patch off the straight of the fabric.

2 Turn the patch over and, using the template as a guide only and without sewing the fabric to the cardboard, tack the semi-circular edge on the wrong side. Follow the shape of the template exactly. Pleat, rather than gather, the spare fabric. Press on the wrong side.

3 The two concave edges are unhemmed but it helps to follow the line of the template with tacking stitches ¼ in (6mm) from the edge. Remove the template.

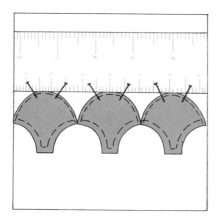

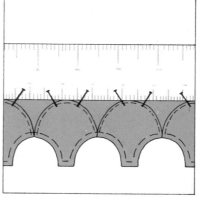

4 Prepare the two rows of patches and assemble them. Pin the first row to a cork board in a straight line, right sides uppermost, with tops of patches lying against a ruler and the patches just touching.

5 Pin the second row below the first to overlap it by ¼ in (6mm), covering the tacked edges of the concave curves. Move the ruler down for each new row of clamshells.

6 Remove pins from one shell; tack to the one next to it. Repeat until all rows are tacked and off board. Hem or slip-stitch the shells together neatly.

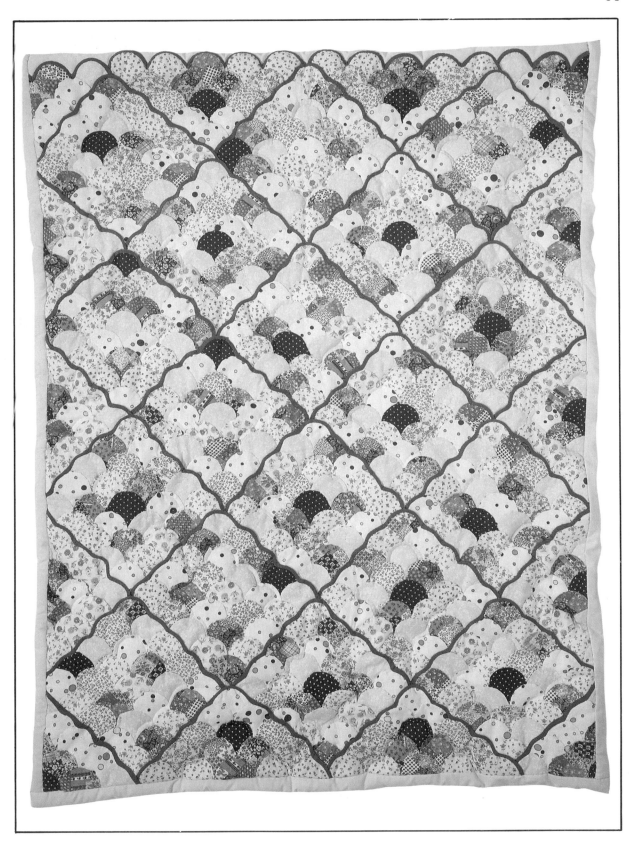

Clamshell quilt by the Guildford quilters, Surrey.

Puff patchwork quilt by Brockham Green WI, Surrey.

Puff patchwork

Puff or biscuit patchwork is made by filling fabric squares (or other shapes) with wadding and sewing them together. The squares can be made as described below or they can be stitched on three sides and stuffed through the fourth side. In that case, pleat at the centre of each side.

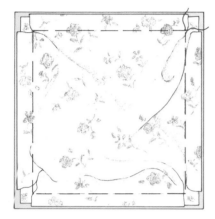

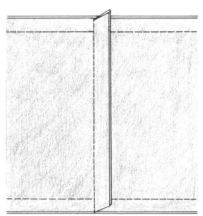

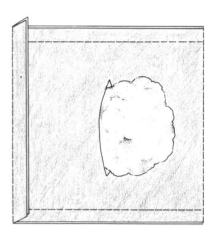

1 Cut two squares, one 1½ times larger than the other. With wrong sides together, pin and tack squares about ¼ in (6mm) from the edge, pleating the corners.

2 Machine-stitch around the four sides of the square where tacked. Join the puffs in rows, so that one side of the quilt is puffed, and all the seams are on the flat side.

3 Cut a small slit in the back of each square and insert wadding through the slit. Stuff squares evenly and not too fully or the quilt will be stiff. Oversew the slits and line the quilt.

Suffolk puff

This variation of puff patchwork is made with gathered circles of fabric. The puffs are sewn together with spaces between them.

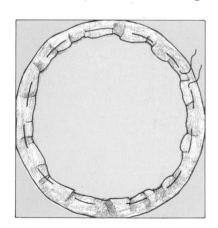

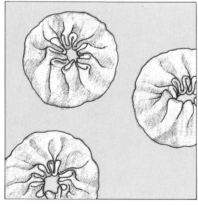

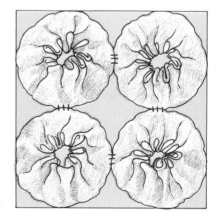

1 Cut circles twice the size of the finished puff. Sew a ¼ in (6mm) hem around the circle in small stitches.

2 Either line with circles of wadding covered with matching fabric or leave unfilled. Draw up the thread tightly.

3 Join the puffs at the back, with a few stitches at the separate points (as shown above).

Folded stars

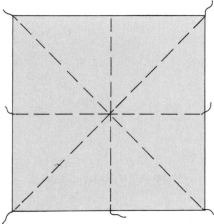

1 Cut a square of cotton backing fabric a little larger than the finished motif will be. 6in (15cm) is a good size. Mark the centre of the backing square; tack lines as shown or mark with pencil.

The technique of making folded stars patchwork (or Somerset patchwork, as it is also called), is not a very well-known one but it is an attractive variation to try. The method involves folding little rectangles of fabric into triangles and sewing them in concentric circles on a backing square, when they will form stars. The backing squares can be cotton or cotton muslin and should be cut a little larger than the finished motif. A 6in (15cm) square is a good size to start with. If the colours of the rows of stars are alternating plain and patterned, they will show up more clearly than if they were all the same.

Every fold should be pressed before the next fold is made and the raw edges of the shapes will be covered by subsequent shapes. If ribbon is used instead of fabric, you do not have to make the first fold.

The size of the circles of stars is a matter of choice and as long as they are neat, there can be as many as four or five circles. They must be placed as accurately as possible and spaced so that they cover the preceding tacking stitches. When this becomes too difficult to achieve due to the increasing size of the circle, the number of stars placed in each round has to be doubled.

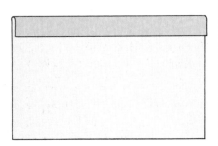

2 Cut four pieces of fabric 2½in × 1½in (6cm × 3.6cm) in a bright colour for the centre. Fold the top edges down ¼in (6mm).

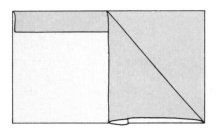

3 Fold down the corners to make a triangle. The folds must be precise, with the edges meeting centrally.

A close-up of the folded stars quilt on page 142

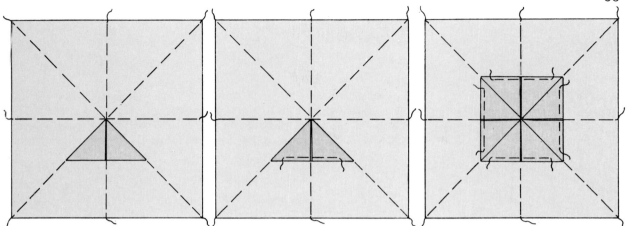

4 Position the first triangle as shown above and bring the needle up through the centre of the foundation square to secure the point of the triangle with a tiny stitch. Secure the thread.

5 Bring the needle up again close to the bottom of the triangle and tack across the base. Do not tack into corners, as these will be trimmed. Keep stitches small, so they will be easy to cover by subsequent rows of triangles. Do not pull the thread too tight, as the work must lie flat.

6 Stitch each of the three remaining triangles the same way, so that their points meet exactly in the centre and their edges meet on four radiating lines from the centre. No backing fabric should show.

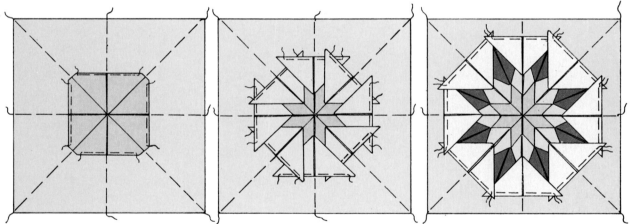

7 Before beginning the next round, trim away the corners of the newly-made square and any other excess fabric outside the tacking stitches, to prevent the work from becoming too bulky.

8 For the second round, cut and fold eight pieces the same size as before but in a contrasting colour or tone. Place each triangle centrally on one of the radiating lines of the foundation square. Stitch and place with precision as before, with all points equidistant from the centre and covering the tacking stitches of the previous row.

9 For the third round, trim away excess fabric and cut 8 more pieces in contrast to the previous layer. Place the points of each new triangle so that they just touch a separate point of the centre star. For the fourth round, place the triangles so that they alternate with those of the third round and cover the previous tacking stitches. When the circle is large enough, the backing fabric can be cut into a circle and the edge bound with bias binding.

Seminole

Note: When joining strips together, sew a seam allowance of ¼ in (6mm) on both edges of the strip.

The name for this type of patchwork comes from the original Seminole Indians of Florida, whose clothing was decorated with bands of coloured fabric. Fabric strips are machine-stitched together, then cut into sections and re-sewn either in straight or

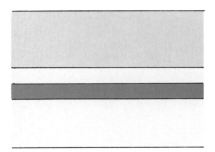

1 Band 1. Sew together two 2in (5cm) strips and two ¾in (2cm) strips, arranged as shown.

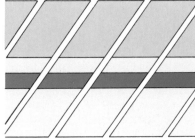

2 Cut in 1¼ in (3cm) diagonal strips at an angle of 55° and sew, offsetting as shown.

3 Trim top and bottom of new band, leaving a ¼ in (6mm) seam allowance.

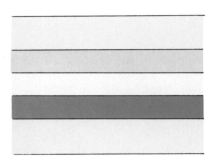

1 Band 2. Sew together two 1½ in (4cm) strips and three 1¼ in (3cm) strips, arranged as shown.

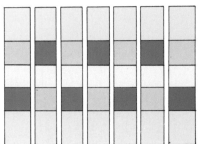

2 Cut in 1¼ in (3cm) strips and sew, offsetting as shown and reversing each alternate strip.

3 Trim top and bottom of new band, leaving a ¼ in (6mm) seam allowance.

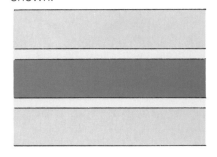

1 Band 3. Sew together three 1½ in (4cm) strips and two ¾ in (2cm) strips, arranged as shown.

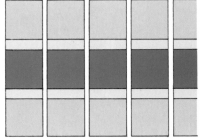

2 Cut in 1½ in (4cm) vertical strips. Cut one ¾ in (2cm) strip in 3¾ in (9.5cm) lengths; sew one to each strip.

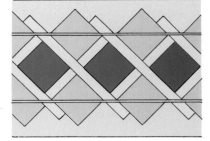

3 Offset vertical strips and sew as shown. Trim, leaving a ¼ in (6mm) seam allowance.

diagonal strips to make patterns. These strips are useful as borders for quilts or as part of an overall design.

After the strips of fabric, which can be any length or width and can be composed of two, three or more strips, have been machined together, all the seams are pressed in the same direction. They are then cut across vertically, again to any length or width and machined again. A great many variations can be made by putting the strips together in different ways.

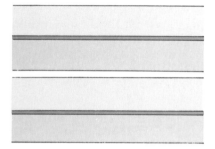 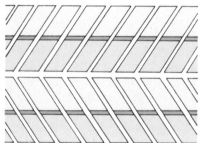 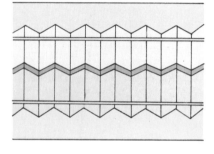

1 Band 4. Sew together two identical bands of two 1½ in (4cm) strips and one ¾ in (2cm) strip as shown.

2 Cut each band into 1¼ in (3cm) strips at an angle of 55°, on opposite diagonals.

3 Sew strips together, alternating one strip from each band, matching seams. Trim top and bottom.

Seminole cushion by Jackie Curtis.

Amish quilts

The Amish are a religious group whose ancestors settled in America in the eighteenth century after being driven out of Switzerland and Germany. To this day they follow the lifestyle of their forebears, without modern trappings such as cars, TV or telephones, shunning outward show and decoration but compensating for this austerity by their love of colour.

Their quilts are simple in design, reflecting their philosophy. There may be a square or a rectangle surrounded by a border or larger square, or bars of different colours, or a log cabin or block design, but the colours are stunning. The quilts are quilted with intricate patterns in fine stitching – it is said that a skilled Amish woman often puts in twenty stitches to an inch.

Although this type of patchwork presents no new techniques, it is of great interest to quilters seriously studying design.

Amish quilt (c. 1915) from Lancaster County, Pennsylvania. (By courtesy of the Robert and Lisa Sainsbury Collection, University of East Anglia, Norwich).

Crazy patchwork

Very popular towards the end of Queen Victoria's reign, this type of patchwork uses scraps of any shape and fabric which are sewn onto a backing. Herringbone and feather stitch were used to decorate all the edges of the patches.

Apart from working out a colour scheme, the design possibilities of this type of patchwork are rather limited. Random-sized and shaped patches are tacked onto the backing, each succeeding patch overlapping the raw edges of its neighbour. Those that are left uncovered are decoratively stitched either by hand or in zigzag or satin machine-stitch.

Crazy patchwork sofa throw from the American Museum, Claverton Manor, Bath, Avon.

SMALL THINGS TO MAKE

These small ideas are for those who may like a change from quiltmaking, or who perhaps lack the time and the inclination to undertake a major piece of work such as a quilt. Making something small can also give you a chance to try out a new design before committing yourself on a grand scale, and it is quite usual for quilters to make a section of a block pattern into a cushion to act as a sort of "traveller's sample" when a quilt is to be sold or raffled.

Here are some colourful ideas for gifts, home brighteners and other things that can be made much more quickly than a quilt, but which use the same techniques.

Left: A white satin cushion with a machine appliqué design of cockle shells, two in blue satin, one in white. The curved shapes of the larger shells are balanced by a long shell in blue satin. Ann Farmer worked the design from photographs of shells, and she finished the cushion by machine-quilting it in flowing lines which are appropriate for the sea theme. Cushion covers always fit better when they are made slightly smaller than the cushion pad they are to fit.

Left: Another sea-theme cushion by Ann Farmer – a cream satin sea horse, machine-appliquéd onto a pink Dupion background. Thin strips of cream satin represent seaweed on either side of the horse.
The background of the cushion is quilted in free-flowing lines, but the sea horse has a more formal quilting design in a grid pattern. Satin cushion covers should be dry cleaned for the best results.

Below: *Two matching hand-pieced patchwork tops, one for a cushion, one for a basket, both edged with broderie anglaise, have a charming, old-fashioned air about them. The design is in hexagons, short diamonds and triangles.*
The same fabrics have been used for the pin cushion on the left with a pink ruched centre.

The ribbon hanger acts as a thimble-holder.
In the background is a miniature four-poster bed with a quilted patchwork bedcover.
In the foreground is a cathedral window pin cushion by Valerie Ibbett. The basket in patchwork-covered cardboard pentagons, and a similarly made hanging decoration made of five short diamonds fitted together,

have their edges ornamented with pins stuck through beads. Everything except the cathedral window pin cushion was made by Jane Walmsley.

Below: This group of hand-sewn patchwork items is by Anthea Linacre. It consists of a tea cozy worked in the clamshell pattern. Silk cord outlines the rounded edges of the outer shells. The grey velvet cushion in the centre is decorated with an eight-pointed star in grey, pink and cream silk, sewn in three rows and appliquéd to the background. The cathedral window patchwork cushion on the right has a cream silk background encasing striped patches in furnishing fabric. The third cushion is worked in a pattern of four groups of silk clamshells applied to pale pink Dupion. Four of the clamshells have embroidered central motifs and the cushion is edged in pale blue cord. The bag in the foreground is made of hexagons in four shades.

Right: This child's waistcoat in strip patchwork by Bridget Long was machined directly onto thin wadding, cut to shape. The strips meet in a chevron at the back. The pink belt, also in strip patchwork, by Valerie Ibbett, is bound with strips of the predominating colour.

Below: A wall-hanging in machine appliqué designed by Pamela Allen. It is lightly padded and makes use of fabrics of different textures. In the foreground is a dog, by Sheila Wilkinson. Machine-pieced squares cover a dog-shaped piece of foam. The dog has hand-sewn ears, felt features and a plaited wool tail.

Left: A machine-sewn, hand-quilted cushion in an interesting design which was first published in 1851, known as "round the twist" or "plaited block". The first block is made of rectangles around a square, the second is an octagon with triangles at each corner. The simple but effective colour scheme is biscuit, rust and brown. Around the edges are squares, triangles, rectangles and trapezoids in matching colours. By Bridget Long.

Left: A bag in black, brown and cream silk, with a hexagon lozenge design, and (centre) a long hexagon drawstring bag in a mixture of fabrics; lined long hexagons form a decorative top. On the right is a Christmas stocking edged with gold cord, worked in red and gold long hexagons. The boxes decorated with an eight-pointed star and a six-pointed star are made of covered, padded and lined cardboard shapes. The stars are applied to the covers and the boxes are decorated with beads. The piped pin cushion (left) is decorated with an applied hexagon rosette; the pin cushion (centre) is a small section of cathedral window patchwork; and the hexagon rosette pin cushion (right) is edged with silk cord. In the foreground, a lined and corded spectacle case is worked in short diamonds which form the "tumbling block" design. All by Anthea Linacre.

Below: A rich and subtle patchwork wall-hanging by Jane Walmsley composed of squares and triangles set within strips, in dark patterned fabrics enlivened by cream. It is hand-sewn and hand-quilted around the patches. The centre squares and the triangles form an octagon.

Left: Two Christmas cards by Brenda Marchbank. A hand-sewn patchwork star in gold and white lamé on black fabric is based on a design of triangles. The "three kings" patchwork, which is also hand-sewn, is decorated with bugles and beads, and it makes a dramatic abstract composition.

Below left: "Tranquillity" is the title of this unusual hand-quilted picture in gold and white lamé, from an original design by Brenda Marchbank. The flowers are Suffolk puffs, made out of glitter nylon, and the leaves are made in machine embroidery on vanishing muslin.

Below: This hand-quilted panel in an abstract design entitled "Flame" forms a striking focal point for a living room. It is made in shot upholstery fabric, with a centre made out of two shades of bronze kid leather. This panel also makes use of little gold beads, gold cord and weaving yarn. Designed and made by Brenda Marchbank.

Above: There are three examples of folded star patchwork in this picture. The lid on the larger basket in the background by Barbara Keeling in shades of green toning to cream has a centre of eight Victorian-type petals around a covered button. The smaller basket, by Jane Walmsley, has folded stars in yellow and green, and the olive green box by Valerie Ibbett has yellows and browns and is lined with yellow satin.

In the foreground is a traditional Durham quilter's pin and thread holder, hand-sewn on papers. The top and base of the holder are 2½in (6cm) hexagons, the base hexagon is stiffened with thin cardboard and the sides are long hexagons fitting the top and base. The ends of the long hexagons fit onto each other to form "ears" through which tape is threaded to hold reels of quilting thread. By Bridget Long. The yellow needlecase by Norah Barnes is made of two felt hexagons, the top one decorated with a hexagon surrounded by six irregular pentagons.

Left: A charming little cathedral window purse, in silk with printed velvet patches in the centre of each square. It has a silk cord tassle and a silk hanging cord. By Anthea Linacre.

Below: Two white lamé evening bags, one hand-quilted with swirling patterns in back-stitch (the pattern is based on a child's building set), the other hand-quilted in running stitch in an interlocking cross design. The belt is decorated with a machine-quilted pattern based on the letter A. It is made of two layers of fabric (top and lining) and is threaded with quilting wool, in Italian or cord quilting, then stiffened.

The bags are made with the usual three layers of quilting fabric and wadding, but they have two extra layers of interlining and fabric. By Brenda Marchbank.

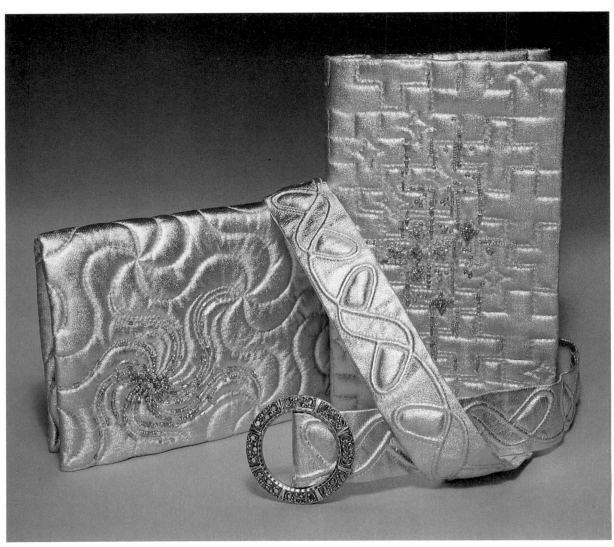

Left: A Christmas wall-hanging by Barbara Keeling, made out of lining fabric backed with thin, non-woven backing. The hanging is hand-sewn and hand-quilted. All the little decorations and gifts on the tree, which are also in patchwork, are attached with press studs, so they can be moved around.

Left: Anthea Linacre's padded box in the red, white and green colours of Christmas, made by covering and lining cardboard shapes. The six-pointed star design applied to the lid has a central corded knob, and the box top is edged with fine red cord.

Right: Red, white and green Christmas decorations to hang on a tree, all measuring only about 3in (7.5cm) across. Each one demonstrates a different design and technique.
They are (left to right, clockwise): log cabin, strip, folded star, six-pointed star, crazy, pieced block, Seminole, cathedral window, Dresden plate and are all hand-pieced and hand-quilted. Made by Pamela Allen.

BEAUTIFUL QUILTS TO MAKE

The beautiful quilts on the following pages were all made by members of the Women's Institute of the U.K. Most of the quilts were made by groups and are the result of planned and concerted effort by several needlewomen, but one or two were the work of one WI member, assisted by two or three helpers.

In this chapter you will find full instructions for making twelve of these quilts which can either be copied exactly or adapted. Templates are actual size, but dimensions of finished quilts are approximate because sewing methods vary. The quantities of fabrics suggested are on the generous side.

Chintz

Dimensions
90in × 55in (229cm × 140cm).

Materials
Floral glazed cotton chintz
    scraps on a white background.
White glazed cotton scraps.
144in × 60in (366cm × 150cm)
    green polyester cotton, for
    lining and borders.
Thin interlining.
Large polystyrene tile.
1in (2.5cm) hexagon template
    and window template.

Cutting guide
Cut in total 1,200 1in (2.5cm)
    hexagons in white, green and
    floral fabric (green for
    borders), with ¼ in (6mm)
    seam allowance (or use a
    window template for floral
    pieces).
Cut interlining slightly larger than
    quilt.
Cut lining from green fabric to
    finished size of quilt plus 1in
    (2.5cm) seam allowances.

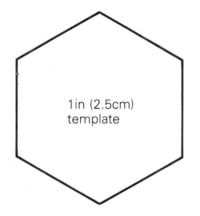

1in (2.5cm)
template

A WI member started making this chintz quilt over ten years ago, and other WI members helped her to finish it, adding two rounds of green patchwork to the sides, interlining the quilt with an old flannelette sheet, backing it and knotting the layers together.

How to work
Make hexagon patches (as described on page 38). Join together in the usual way, setting the hexagons with flat top. This creates an attractive zigzag pattern along the sides of the quilt. Make sure that the flowers and leaves are in scale with each other and with the size of the hexagon.

When making the wreath of flowers in the centre of the quilt, pin each bunch of flowers on a large polystyrene tile so that you can arrange large flowers in the middle surrounded by buds and leaves, keeping the wreath roughly the same width.

Surround floral patches with white patches. Then finish the edge of the quilt with one and a half rows of green hexagon patches in lining fabric.

Tack the interlining to the top, and with right sides together seam the lining to the top, leaving one edge unseamed for turning. Then turn and stitch the unseamed edge.

Knot the three layers of quilt together at regular intervals, on the joins of the patches. (See page 63 for knotting.)

Close-up of the chintz quilt opposite.

Chintz quilt made by Stoke Fleming WI, Devon.

Dresden plate

Dimensions
100in × 78in (253cm × 198cm).

Materials
Colour A: 252in × 45in (640cm × 115cm) polyester cotton, for appliquéd squares, lattices and binding.
Colour B: 162in × 45in (415cm × 115cm) polyester cotton, for diamonds, lattices and borders.
Colour C: 36in × 45in (90cm × 115cm) polyester cotton, for squares.
Colour D: 234in × 45in (595cm × 115cm) polyester cotton, for lining.
12in (30cm) strips of 19 polyester cotton prints, for petals.
144in × 60in (366cm × 150cm) Terylene wadding.

Cutting guide
Colour A: 12 17in (43cm) squares and 31 17in × 2½in (43cm × 6.5cm) lattices; 1½in (4cm)-wide bias strips to bind edges of quilt.
Colour B: 48 pieces from template 2; 62 17in × 3in (43cm × 7.5cm) lattices; 2 borders 100in × 4¾in (253.5cm × 12cm) and 2 borders 78½in × 4¾in (199cm × 12cm).
Colour C: 20 6½in (16.5cm) squares.
Colour D: 12 linings to fit finished blocks (see diagram overleaf) plus 1½in (4cm) each side (for overlapping and ½in/1.25cm seam allowances) and 4 linings for borders.
From prints, 355 pieces from template 1.
12 waddings slightly larger than blocks (see diagram); 4 waddings for borders.

This quilt is based on a design by Gladys Boult. It fits a double bed; the quilting and appliqué work was hand-sewn.

How to work
Cut out the shapes from the fabric, using templates where appropriate – add ¼in (6mm) all round when using templates, for seam allowances. Seam together by machine the lattices, small squares and large squares to make the blocks (½in/1.25cm seam allowances are included in measurements). Seam together the petals of the Dresden plates.

Turn under and tack into place the hems on the inner and outer edges of the Dresden plates, ensuring that all twelve are of the same size.

Centre the plates on each large square, tack into place, then secure by hand with ladder-stitch or slip-stitch.

Place and apply the four diamonds in the shape of a cross in the centre of each plate by hand with ladder-stitch or slip-stitch.

Mark out where you wish to quilt on each block with chalk marks or by tacking around templates (see the quilting diagram overleaf).

Pin and tack together the three layers to be quilted (top, wadding and lining). Quilt each block. Do not quilt on the seam allowance.

The borders are made of strips in Colour B with appliquéd petals at regular intervals, creating a slightly scalloped edge. Make a border strip for the top of the quilt, one for the bottom and one for each side. At each end of each side border strip appliqué a series of petals to make a fan-shaped corner, trimming slightly the narrow ends of the petals.

Waddings for the borders should be cut in strips to the required lengths and later trimmed to fit the scalloped edges of the quilt. Linings for the borders should be cut with 1in (2.5cm) seam allowances on the inside and cut to cover the scalloped edges on the outside and then be trimmed to within ½in (1.25cm) of the edge of the quilt (the seam allowances will be hidden by binding). Tack the border wadding and lining strips to the borders and quilt through all three layers close to the seams of the petals, without quilting on the seam allowances.

Assemble the twelve blocks (see diagram overleaf for the arrangement of the blocks), joining top layers by machining, trimming the wadding to butt, and slip-stitching the lining fabric layers, overlapping these and turning under only the top edges ½in (1.25cm).

Join the border sections to the main section of the quilt, stitching the top layers first, then trimming the wadding to butt and slip-stitching the lining fabric layers, overlapping these and turning under only the top edges ½in (1.25cm). Trim the edges of the wadding to fit the scalloped edges of the quilt. Attach the binding to the front of the quilt by machine, then turn over, trim and slip-stitch the binding into place on the back, covering the raw edges with the binding.

Dresden plate quilt made by Cuddington WI, Buckinghamshire.

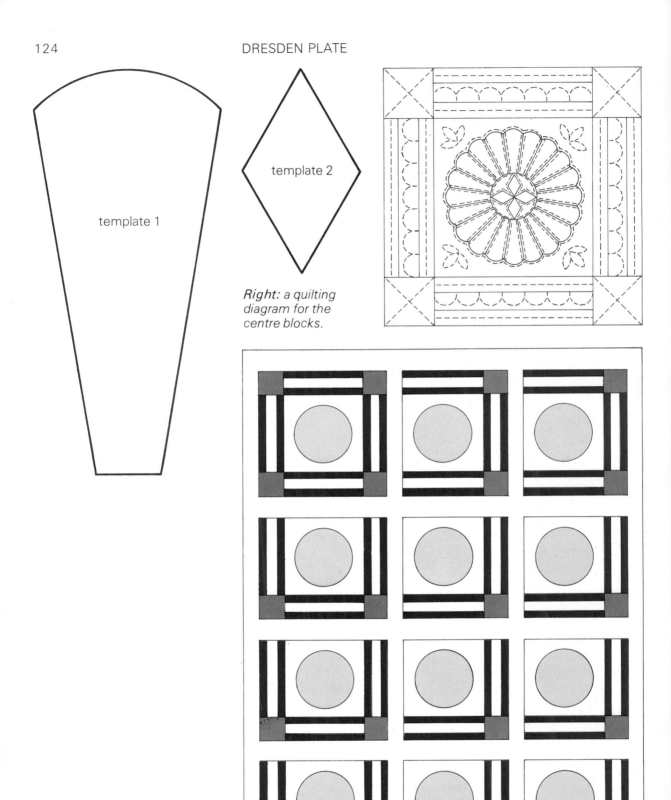

template 1

template 2

Right: a quilting diagram for the centre blocks.

Right: This diagram shows how the blocks are assembled. Sew the finished blocks in columns of four, then sew the vertical columns together.

Grandmother's cross

This attractive quilt was made mainly in furnishing fabric, using a floral-and-striped fabric and cutting it so that both flowers and stripes were used. Separate amounts of floral and striped fabric are given for the quilt described here, instead of the floral-and-striped fabric originally used. These are teamed up with patterned and plain fabrics. The colours are arranged so as to give a checkerboard effect.

How to work

Cut the cardboard templates as in the pattern overleaf. Place the template on the wrong side of the fabric and draw around it in pencil but when cutting, allow at least ¼in (6mm) all around for seam allowances. Remember that you will be cutting eight pieces from template 2 for each block, four with the template the right way up and four with it reversed, for the opposite side of the block. Finished blocks are approximately 12in (30cm) and for this size of quilt, you will need 35 blocks (five across and seven down). Remember that there are two designs for the blocks (see the diagrams overleaf) and these are placed alternately to achieve a checkerboard effect.

Place patches right sides together with pencilled stitching lines matching, then sew along the line with small, straight running stitches. Begin and end each row of stitches with a back-stitch to secure. Do not sew through the seam allowance.

The centre of each block is composed of squares. Join the rows to form a square using a butted seam, which enables you to press the seam in any direction you wish.

Stitch the outer border of each block in four strips (see the diagrams overleaf). (Remember that you should have cut with template 2 four the right way up and four reversed for each block.) Sew each strip alongside the central section, with butted seams as before. When all four strips are joined, join the mitres at each corner.

Sew the short lattices to the blocks, assembling the blocks in columns. Put the long lattices between the columns and sew together the short lattices, the blocks and the long lattices. Join the short lattices, the blocks and the long lattices to the border lattices, mitring the corners of the border lattices. Add the border, mitring the corners. (See the diagram overleaf.)

The quilt is finished off by lining it first with a layer of thin Terylene wadding, slip-stitched around the edge, then the lining. When cutting the lining, cut one piece the length of the quilt and the whole width of the fabric with seam allowances, then join on two strips, one on either side, which are also the length of the quilt with seam allowances, to avoid a centre seam. The wadding will also need to be cut in strips and joined. Attach both wadding and lining at intervals to the front of the quilt with small stitches.

Bind the edges of the quilt with 1in (2.5cm) strips of lining fabric, machining the binding to the right sides of the quilt. Trim the edges, turn and hem all around onto the lining, mitring the corners.

Dimensions
96in × 70in (244cm × 178cm).

Materials
Colour A: 108in × 48in (275cm × 120cm) cotton.
Colour B: 117in × 48in (300cm × 120cm) cotton.
Colour C: 117in × 48in (300cm × 120cm) cotton.
Colour D: 96in × 48in (244cm × 120cm) cotton, for lattices.
Colour E: 207in × 48in (525cm × 120cm) cotton, for lining and edges.
207in × 37in (525cm × 94cm) thin Terylene wadding.

Cutting guide
For 1st block:
Colour A: 4 pieces from template 1 and 5 from 3.
Colour B: 4 pieces from template 3.
Colour C: 4 pieces from template 2 and 4 *in reverse*.

For 2nd block:
Colour A: 4 pieces from template 2 and 4 *in reverse*.
Colour B: 4 pieces from template 3.
Colour C: 4 pieces from template 1 and 5 from 3.
Colour B: 4 3in (7.5cm)-wide borders (½in/1.25cm seam allowances included) to fit quilt plus seam allowances.
Colour D: 2in (5cm)-wide lattices (½in/1.25cm seam allowances included): 30 short lattices to width of block plus seam allowances; 4 long lattices to length of blocks plus short lattices, plus seam allowances; 4 border lattices with seam allowances.
Colour E: See *How to work*; 1in (2.5cm)-wide strips for edges.
Wadding slightly larger than quilt.

Grandmother's cross quilt made by Onchan WI, Isle of Man.

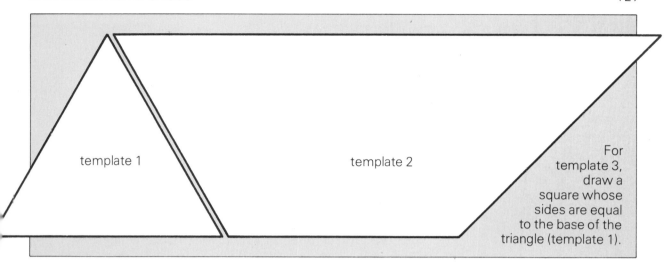

template 1

template 2

For template 3, draw a square whose sides are equal to the base of the triangle (template 1).

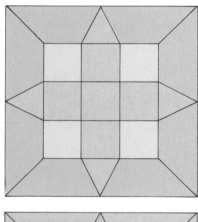

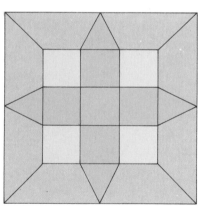

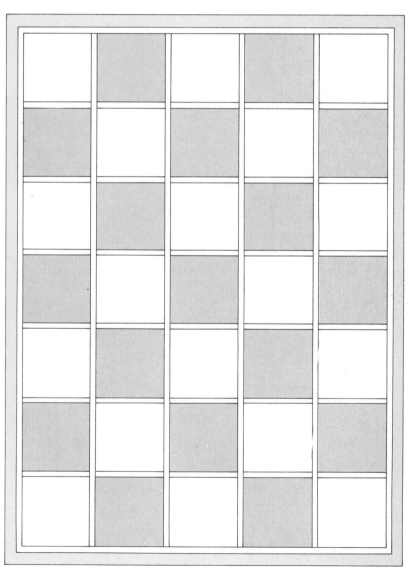

Above: First block (top) and second block (bottom).
1, 2 and 3 are templates.
Right: Diagram showing the arrangement of blocks to achieve the checkerboard effect, and position of lattices and borders.

Zigzags

Dimensions
68in × 54in (173cm × 138cm).

Materials
Colour A: 79in × 45in (200cm × 115cm) polyester cotton.
Colour B: 20in × 45in (50cm × 115cm) polyester cotton in 9 shades.
Colour C: 81in × 36in (206cm × 90cm) polyester cotton, for border (amount depends on pattern chosen).
Colour D: 75in × 60in (190cm × 150cm) polyester cotton, for lining.
138in × 37in (350cm × 94cm) or 70in × 60in (178cm × 150cm) Terylene wadding.

Cutting guide
Colours A and B: Pieces from template for zigzags (304 whole triangles and 32 half triangles).
Colour C: 7in (18cm)-wide borders (½in/1.25cm seam allowances included) to required lengths plus ½in (1.25cm) seam allowances.
Colour D: Lining to finished size of quilt plus 1in (2.5cm) seam allowances.
Wadding (in strips if necessary) slightly larger than quilt.

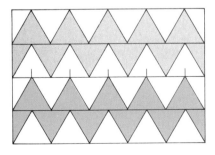

How the sections fit together, and tacking-stitch markers.

Nine WI members were involved in making this quilt with its design of green and white zigzags.

The subtle colour scheme was inspired by the green broad-striped border fabric, and the other greens and the white fabric were purchased to go with it.

The design is an American one, and is based on a series of triangles, placed in rows.

How to work
Cut paper templates for zigzags from the template below – add ¼in (6mm) all around for seam allowance when cutting the fabric. Note that the zigzags in Colours B shade from light to dark, separated by zigzags in Colour A. Sew the triangle templates in sections as in the diagram. There are seven complete sections and two half sections, one at the top and one at the bottom. After completing each section, press it well.

Mark the half-way point along the base of each triangle at the bottom of each section with tacking thread. Join sections of zigzags together with points of successive triangles matching the threads on the triangle above. Remove the papers and press well.

Sew on the borders, mitring the corners.

Tack the wadding and the lining in place. (Join the wadding if necessary.) Quilt the zigzags in Colour A ¼in (6mm) in from the seam and quilt the border.

Trim the wadding. Turn under the border and lining edges and slip-stitch together.

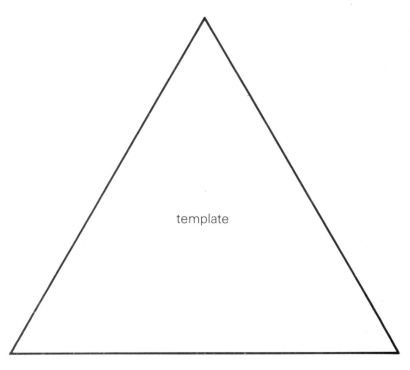

template

A striking zigzag-patterned quilt by Old Catton (Evening) WI, Norfolk.

Double wedding ring

Dimensions
43in × 36in (110cm × 90cm).

Materials
Colour A: 117in × 36in (300cm × 90cm) cotton, for patches, lining and bias binding.
Colour B: 20in × 36in (50cm × 90cm) cotton, add extra if patterned.
Colour C: 20in × 36in (50cm × 90cm) cotton, add extra if patterned.
Colour D: 29in × 36in (75cm × 90cm) cotton, add extra if patterned.
Colour E: 12in × 36in (30cm × 90cm) cotton, minimum.
Colour F: 12in × 36in (30cm × 90cm) cotton, minimum.
40in × 48in (100cm × 120cm) lightweight Terylene wadding.
Embroidery thread for quilting.
Approximately 171in (450cm) fine piping cord.

Cutting guide
For twenty rings cut:
Colour A: 20 pieces from template 4 and lining to finished size of quilt plus 1in (2.5cm) for seam allowances. Bias binding strips.
Colour B: 50 pieces from template 2 and 25 pieces from template 5.
Colour C: 48 pieces from template 2 and 24 pieces from template 5.
Colour D: 98 pieces from template 1 and 98 pieces from template 1 *but in reverse.*
Colour E: 49 pieces from template 3.
Colour F: 49 pieces from template 3.
Wadding slightly larger than quilt.

There were several good reasons for choosing the traditional "double wedding ring" pattern for this cot quilt. First, it could be broken down into small units to enable a group of people to work on it at the same time. Secondly, the resulting design was a good one for quilting, and thirdly, the pattern was difficult enough to satisfy high competition standards.

The team of fifteen workers made trial sections of the quilt to pinpoint problem areas and to balance the size and colour harmonies before they began. They settled on a cot-sized quilt to reduce costs, in a basic turquoise colour, and they worked in cotton fabrics for greater accuracy. All the fabrics used were well washed and ironed before use to make sure they would neither shrink nor stretch and that all the colours were completely fast.

Accuracy is essential for all patchwork but particularly so for this pattern and to achieve it, the team produced master templates from which all lining papers and fabric pieces were cut, constantly referring back to them at all stages of sewing.

The most difficult stages were the joining of the large pieces, with their fine tapering points, to the patchwork ovals, making sure that colours were arranged in the correct sequence, and piping the edges.

How to work
You will need twenty-four horizontal oval sections and twenty-five vertical oval sections altogether, to attach to the twenty central sections (template 4). When joining these sections together, follow the colour interchanges as shown overleaf.

Cut the templates as in the pattern overleaf, adding ¼in (6mm) for turnings when cutting the fabric.

Follow the general instructions for pieced patchwork on pages 36–9 to fit the pieces together, paying special attention to precision of cutting, fitting and sewing. Check all lining papers and fabric pieces against original templates all the time to ensure that the pattern works.

Check the colour sequence of the individual patches before sewing them together, by following the diagram overleaf.

First join together the outer segments (templates 1, 2 and 3). Join these segments to the centre of the oval (template 5). Join completed ovals to fabric cut from template 4. Then join completed sections to each other, still observing the colour sequence.

When the patchwork is complete, remove the papers except at the edges of the quilt, keeping these in place until the last possible moment to give the work firmness. Tack patchwork to wadding and lining but do not trim wadding or lining yet, as it is better to trim it a little at a time when you come to do the piping.

Quilt in small running stitches, where shown on the diagram overleaf. To finish the edges, make bias strips from the lining fabric and cover the piping cord with it. (See page 77 for piping.) Use fine piping cord for this quilt.

Remove the papers from the outside row of patches. Turn under the seam allowance on the edges and tack the covered

Double wedding ring quilt made by members of Southwell WI, Nottinghamshire.

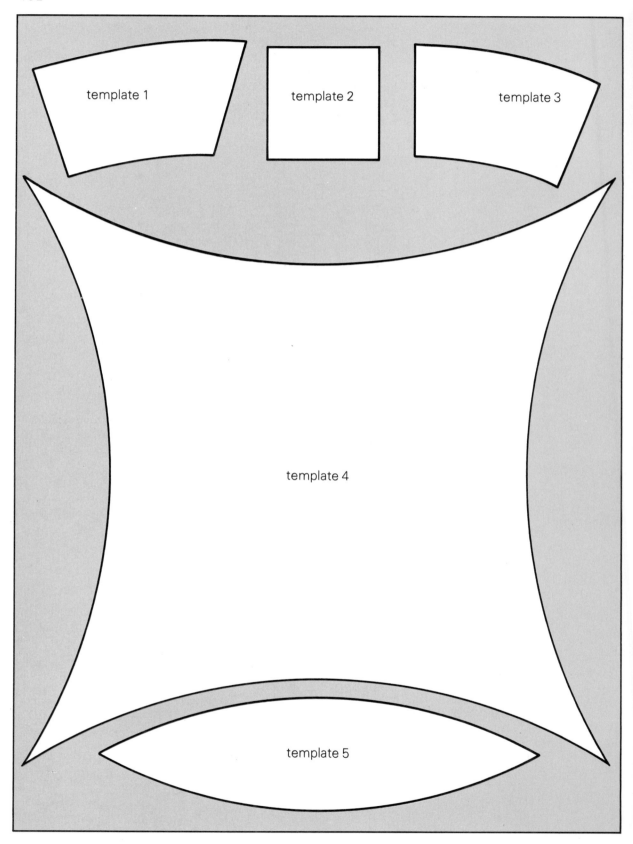

template 1

template 2

template 3

template 4

template 5

piping cord to the wrong side of the patch edge, through the seam, cord cover and wadding, leaving the lining free. When tacked and eased satisfactorily around the curves and into tight corners, stitch the piping in place with small running stitches.

Trim back the wadding as close to the piping cord as possible. Trim the lining to shape, allowing ⅜in (1cm) for turning. Cut in gradually as you hem along. Turn under and hem to back of covered piping cord.

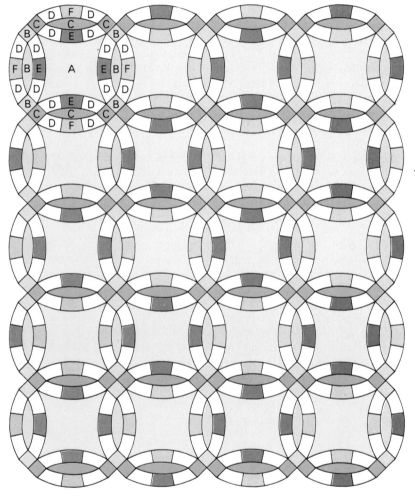

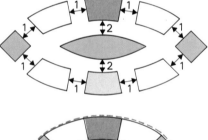

Left: The chart shows the interchange of colours on the circles.
Below: The assembly sequence of each oval and the positioning of the quilting.

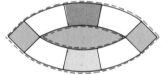

Variation

The double wedding ring pattern is a versatile one and can be used in patchwork (as in the quilt illustrated on these pages) or as an appliqué motif. When using the rings as applied motifs, the circles are made in patchwork sections in the usual way, then they are looped together just before completion and can be hemmed as one onto a plain background.

In the arrangement shown here both rings are completed and one is sewn to the other before being applied. An alternative is to loop the second ring through the first, then join it up and then apply it to the background, giving a slightly raised effect.

In spite of looking so complicated, this patchwork ring design is a simple repeat, needing only one set of templates.

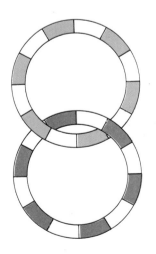

Grandmother's fan

Dimensions
96in × 66in (243cm × 167cm).

Materials
Colour A: 324in × 45in (825cm × 115cm) cotton (includes lining and binding).
Colour B: 126in × 45in (320cm × 115cm) cotton.
Colour C: 126in × 36in (320cm × 90cm) cotton.
12in (30cm) strips of 8 patterned fabrics.
432in (1,100cm) edging lace.
270in × 37in (685cm × 94cm) or 198in × 60in (500cm × 150cm) Terylene wadding.

Cutting guide
Colour A: 24 pieces from template 2; lining to size of finished quilt (in strips) plus 1in (2.5cm) seam allowances; bias binding strips.
Colour B: 24 pieces from template 3 (see *How to work*).
Colour C: 18 short lattices 14in × 3in (35.5cm × 7.5cm) (½in/1.25cm seam allowances included); 5 long lattices 59in × 3in (149.5cm × 7.5cm) (½in/1.25cm seam allowances included); 2 borders 97in × 5in (240.5cm × 12.5cm) (½in/1.25cm seam allowances included); 2 borders 67in × 5in (169.5cm × 12.5cm) (½in/1.25cm seam allowances included).
24 pieces from each of 8 patterned fabrics from template 1.
Lace to edge fans.
Wadding (in strips if necessary) slightly larger all around than quilt.

Right: Two quilting patterns suitable for fans.

Twelve WI members made this quilt in a colour scheme of pink, lavender and blue. There are twenty-four blocks and each person made two, quilting them to their own design. Lavender-coloured lattices join the blocks. The quilting of the lattices and the border was done on a large frame so that six people could work on it.

How to work
Make templates 1 and 2. Cut pieces from these templates to make twenty-four fan sections (there are eight patterned fabrics for each fan) – add ¼in (6mm) all around for seam allowances when cutting the fabric. Join the eight patterned segments together, then join to the pieces cut from template 2.

Each block is 13in (33cm) square. Using the fan section for the left-hand lower corner of each block, make another template (not shown) which becomes template 3, to fit the rest of the block. When using template 3 to cut the pieces from the fabric, remember to add ¼in (6mm) all around for seam allowances. Attach the pieces cut from template 3 as follows: machine ¼in (6mm) in from the curved edge. Snip to within a hair's breadth of the stitching: this will allow the curve to lie flat.

Appliqué the lace along the top edge of each fan.

There are four blocks across and six blocks down in this quilt. Join the short lattices to the blocks in six rows. Then join the long lattices to the rows of blocks and short lattices. Attach the border to the blocks, short lattices and long lattices, mitring the corners.

Join the strips of wadding together. Join the strips of lining together. Prepare the quilt for quilting on a frame as shown in the quilting chapter, placing the three layers (top, wadding and lining) together and tacking them firmly. Quilt along the seams of each section of each fan. Quilt the areas of each block outside the fan, and the lattices and border.

Attach the bias binding to the front of the quilt, then turn and slip-stitch into place on the back.

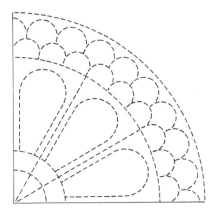
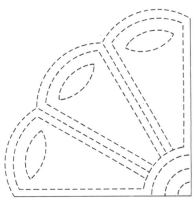

Grandmother's fan quilt made by Llanfoist WI, Gwent.

Right: An alternative design can be made by arranging fans in the pattern shown here.

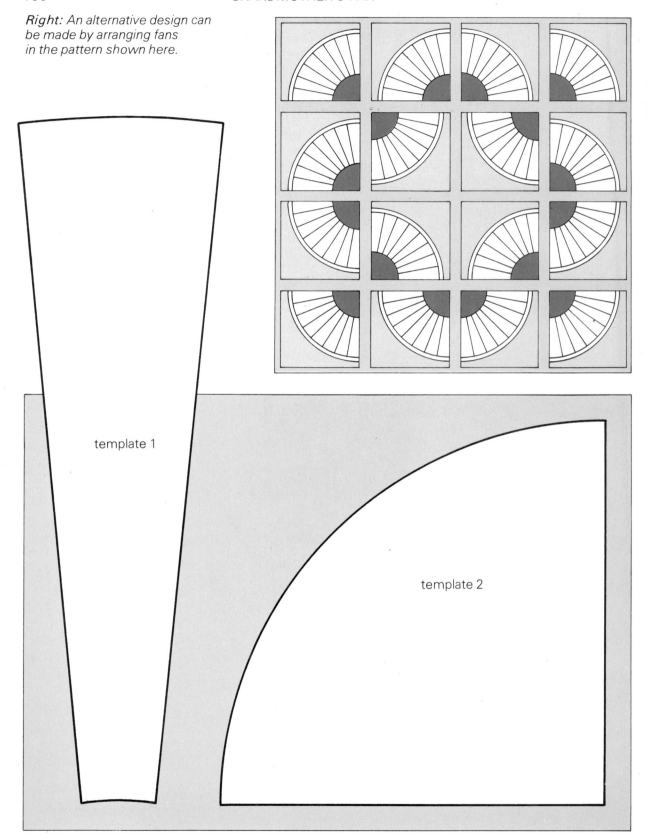

template 1

template 2

Bird pictures

This quilt is based on an American design called "Salt Lake City", but it uses the pieced patchwork method of sewing around papers and oversewing on the wrong side.

Twenty WI members made up the fifty-six blocks, which measured approximately 12in (30cm) square, and the blocks were placed seven in width and eight in length.

How to work
Cut the pieces, allowing ¼in (6mm) all around for seam allowances when cutting with templates from the fabric and using the window template to ensure that the pictures are central.

Join the block components as in the diagram below, in pieced patchwork style. Twenty blocks have pieces from template 2 in Colour B and thirty-six have pieces from template 2 in Colour D. Assemble the quilt top, placing the blocks with Colour D at the outside edges of the quilt, interspersing the blocks with Colour B at random among blocks with Colour D.

Remove the papers. Join the wadding and tack the quilt top to the wadding and the lining. Tie the lining to the front and the wadding with a knot at the centre of each large picture with matching linen thread.

Trim the wadding. Machine-stitch the edge of the binding to the right side of the quilt, then turn and slip-stitch to the lining.

Dimensions
96in × 84in (244cm × 214cm).

Materials
Colour A: 108in × 60in (275cm × 150cm) polyester cotton.
Colour B: 160in × 90in (400cm × 229cm) polyester cotton (this includes lining).
Colour C: 117in × 45in (300cm × 115cm) polyester cotton.
Colour D: 97in × 36in (247cm × 90cm) polyester cotton (this includes binding).
240in × 37in (610cm × 94cm) Terylene wadding.
A 7in (17.5cm) window template with a 6in (15cm) aperture.

Cutting guide
Colour A: 448 pieces from template 1; 56 6in (15cm) squares using window template.
Colour B: 80 pieces from template 2; 224 pieces from template 4; lining to finished size of quilt plus ½in (1.25cm) seam allowances.
Colour C: 224 pieces from template 3; 224 pieces from template 4.
Colour D: 144 pieces from template 2; bias or straight 3in (7.5cm)-wide binding strips (½in/1.25cm seam allowance included).
Lining papers for each piece cut to template size.
Wadding (in strips if necessary) slightly larger than quilt.

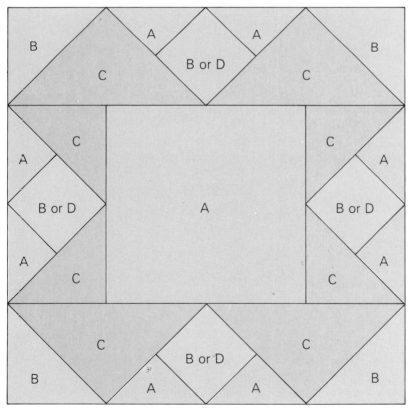

This diagram shows how one block is constructed.

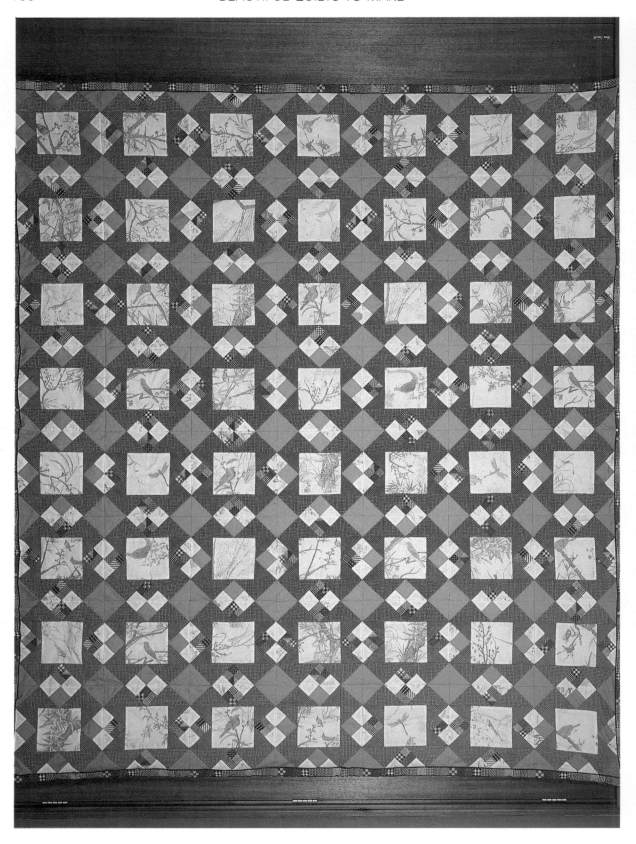

Bird pictures quilt by Billington and Langho WI, Lancashire.

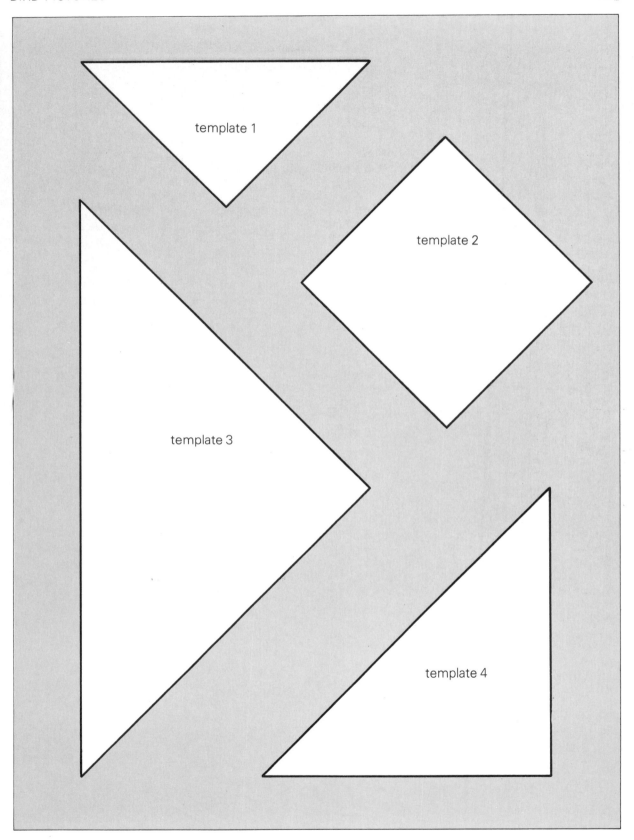

Red blocks

Dimensions
91in × 72in (232cm × 184cm).

Materials
Colour A: 276in × 48in (700cm × 120cm) polyester cotton (this includes lining).
Colour B: 158in × 48in (400cm × 120cm) polyester cotton (this includes border).
Colour C: 39in × 48in (100cm × 120cm) polyester cotton.
Colour D: 39in × 48in (100cm × 120cm) polyester cotton.
Colour E: 39in × 48in (100cm × 120cm) polyester cotton (this includes piping).
Embroidery silk.

Cutting guide
Colour A: 6 20in (51cm) squares (½in/1.25cm seam allowances included); 36 pieces from the template given; lining in two pieces to finished size of quilt plus 1in (2.5cm) seam allowances.
Colour B: 6 20in (51cm) squares (½in/1.25cm seam allowances included); 8½in (21.5cm)-wide borders (½in/1.25cm seam allowances included) to required lengths plus ½in (1.25cm) seam allowances.
Colour C: 36 pieces from template.
Colour D: 36 pieces from template.
Colour E: 36 pieces from template; bias or straight strips for piping around quilt without border.

Sixteen WI members worked on this quilt, which features squares with a three-dimensional box design alternating with squares with a stitching design in embroidery silk. The workers used striped fabric for part of the three-dimensional box design. It is particularly important when using striped fabric to see that it is placed correctly, with the stripes running in the right direction.

How to work
There are twelve 19in (48.5cm) blocks, three across and four down. Six blocks feature the three-dimensional patchwork design. Using the template below, cut the pieces for the three-dimensional box design for each of the six blocks, remembering to add ¼in (6mm) all around when cutting from the fabric. It is the use of three diamonds in three tones (light, medium and dark) which gives the three-dimensional effect (see page 14). Join the pieces for each design and appliqué the design to the centre of each of the squares in Colour B.

Six blocks are in Colour A and these feature a stitching design. Stitch with the three threads of stranded embroidery silk in two rows of running stitch. The design for this stitching is a square diamond within a larger square diamond. Start sewing the outer square diamond at the mid-point of one of the sides of the block and take the stitches to the mid-point of the next three sides in turn. Sew another square diamond within the large square diamond.

Join the blocks, alternating blocks that have the three-dimensional box design with blocks that have stitching. Pipe the outer edges of this section of the quilt.

Add the border, turning under the ½in (1.25cm) seam allowances and mitring the corners.

Join the lining strips (the join will be down the centre of the quilt). Add the lining to the top quilt. (There is no wadding.)

Machine-quilt on the mitred corners of the quilt.

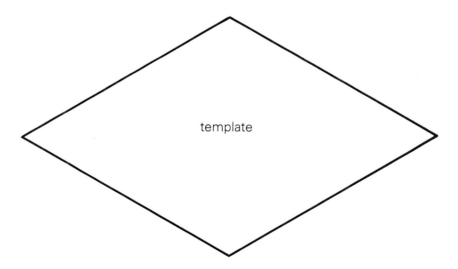

template

Red blocks quilt by Laycock and District WI, Yorkshire.

Folded stars quilt by Aldbourne WI, Wiltshire.

Folded stars

"Folded stars" or "Somerset patchwork" is an intricate method which involves folding small rectangles of fabric into triangles and sewing each one onto a circular background to make roundels. For this quilt, thirty-five roundels were mounted on square patches, divided by lattices and arranged five across and seven down. The original quilt included a border made up of different-coloured triangles with a mini-roundel at each corner which is not shown in the photograph and therefore not described here.

Each of the fourteen workers took home one plain square, one circle of muslin and eight strips of either brown or green different fabrics at a time to make up; each one was given a free hand with the choice and arrangement of her fabrics, so no two roundels are alike. However, the workers limited their colours to four plain and four patterned browns and greens.

How to work
Make the roundels on their muslin foundation circles. (The technique for making folded stars is described on page 98.) Machine-sew the bias binding to the right side of the roundel edges, then turn and slip-stitch in place.

Hand-sew the roundels to the squares, which will measure 10in (25cm) when finished.

Join seven squares with their roundels in a column, alternating the colours of the roundels, with short lattices separating the squares. Make five columns in this way, bearing in mind that you should start the next column with Colour A if you started the first column with Colour B or vice versa, so that the roundels will be alternately placed in different colours in the rows of the quilt as well as the columns.

Sew the five completed columns to the long lattices. Sew on the top and bottom lattices. (Lattice corners are not mitred in this quilt.)

Join the wadding strips. Tack the wadding and the lining to the top of the quilt. Turn under the lining and turn under the top of the quilt and slip-stitch them together.

Hand-quilt round each of the thirty-five squares.

Dimensions
90in × 65in (227cm × 164cm).

Materials
Colour A: 35in × 36in (89cm × 90cm) each of four plain cottons; 45in × 36in (115cm × 90cm) each of four patterned cottons; 48in × 90in (120cm × 228cm) polyester cotton sheeting; 468in (1,200cm) bias binding.
Colour B: 35in × 36in (89cm × 90cm) each of four plain cottons: 45in × 36in (115cm × 90cm) each of four patterned cottons; 468in (1,200cm) bias binding.
Colour C: 180in × 90in (457cm × 228cm) polyester cotton sheeting (this includes lining).
36in × 60in (100cm × 150cm) muslin.
200in × 48in (508cm × 115cm) Terylene wadding.

Cutting guide
Colours A & B: plain and patterned cottons: 2½in × 1½in (6.5cm × 4cm) pieces.
Colour A: polyester cotton: 2 66in × 3½in (166.5cm × 9cm) lattices for top and bottom of quilt (½in/1.25cm seam allowances included); 6 long lattices 86in × 3½in (216.5cm × 9cm) (½in/1.25cm seam allowances included); 30 short lattices 11in × 3½in (27.5cm × 9cm) (½in/1.25cm seam allowances included).
Colour C: 35 11in (27.5cm) squares (½in/1.25cm seam allowances included); lining to fit finished quilt plus 1in/2.5cm seam allowances).
35 7in (18cm)-diameter muslin circles.
Wadding (in strips if necessary) slightly larger than quilt.

Close-ups of the brown and green roundels.

Hexagon lozenge

Dimensions
38in × 28in (97cm × 71cm).

Materials
Colours A and B: 4in (10cm)
  strips of various
  cottons/polyester cottons,
  with enough of two fabrics
  (one of each colour) to make
  lozenge intersections (see
  How to work) and enough of
  one of these to make lining.
43in × 37in (110cm × 94cm)
  Terylene wadding.
18 very small matching buttons.
½in (1.25cm) hexagon
  templates plus window
  templates.
Narrow lace to edge quilt at front
  and back (optional).

Cutting guide
Colours A and B: ½in (1.25cm)
  hexagons in assorted fabrics,
  with enough hexagons in two
  fabrics (one of each colour) to
  make lozenge intersections,
  with ¼in (6mm) seam
  allowances (or use a window
  template).
Lining from one of fabrics used
  in lozenge intersections to
  size of finished quilt plus 1in
  (2.5cm) seam allowances.
Wadding slightly larger than
  quilt.

template

This cot quilt is made up of tiny hexagons (there are about 2,300 in all). It was produced by one person, with help from other WI members who provided fabrics and ideas about colour and design. A flat display table was useful when planning the design.

How to work
Make hexagon patches as described on page 38. Hexagons are assembled in groups of 49 in a lozenge shape (the pattern is on page 13). This lozenge is the motif of the quilt. Each lozenge has a different arrangement of two basic colours, and there are thirteen complete lozenges.

Once all the motifs are made, place them on a flat table and move them around until the best layout is reached. Then make the corner and edging groups of hexagons, bearing in mind that intersections consisting of two rows of hexagons will join the motifs and corner and edging sections. All hexagons are "whole" except at the edges of the quilt, where they are folded in half after removal of papers.

Join the motifs and corner and edging groups of hexagons with two rows of hexagons, one in each of the basic colours.

To finish the quilt, interline with the wadding, trimmed to fit, and back with the lining. Fold the lining to the front of the quilt and hem in place. Attach the lining to the quilt top with very tiny matching buttons at the lozenge intersections.

Rows of narrow lace can be sewn around the back and front edges to cover hemming stitches.

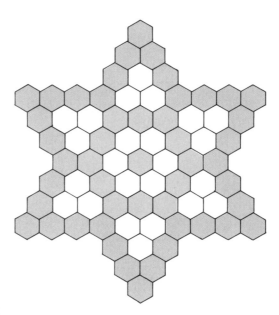

Variation
A "grandmother's flower garden" design with additional groups of three hexagons on all six sides, forming a star, would make an attractive alternative to the central hexagon shapes opposite.

Hexagon quilt by Shenstone WI, Staffordshire.

BEAUTIFUL QUILTS TO MAKE

Mariner's compass

Dimensions
83in × 83in (210cm × 210cm).

Materials
Colour A: 216in × 36in (550cm × 90cm) cotton.
Colour B: 36in × 36in (90cm × 90cm) cotton.

The WI members who made this striking quilt preferred to make a medallion rather than a block quilt. This quilt is hand-sewn, in shades of pink, blue, maroon and grey and quilted on a quilting frame, and it has a "mariner's compass" design. The whole quilt after the second border was made up of a series of borders. The lining was brought around to the front to edge the quilt.

Mariner's compass quilt by Llantilio Pertholey WI, Gwent.

How to work

Use templates 1, 2, 3, 5 and 9 to cut the pieces required for the "mariner's compass", allowing ¼in (6mm) all around for seam allowances. In this quilt the colours are as follows: Colour A represents cream; B is dark red; C and D are patterned in shades of pinks and blues; E is striped red and blue and F is maroon. Make up the "mariner's compass", then appliqué it to the centre square cut from Colour A. Edge the square with a border cut from Colour E, mitring the corners. Set the square diagonally and square off the sides with triangles from Colour A, cut with ½in (1.25mm) seam allowances.

The second border is made from templates 6 to 8 ("flying geese" and squares within squares) – add ¼in (6mm) for seam allowances. There are 72 "geese". A goose is made up of fabric cut from template 6 (one piece) and template 7 (two pieces), sewn together to make an oblong (see the photograph opposite). Squares within squares are positioned at the corners and halfway along each side. There are nine "geese" each side of a square within a square, and the direction in which they "point" varies (see the photograph opposite). A square within a square is made up of a square set diagonally, with its sides squared off by four triangles. Template 8 (one piece) and template 7 (four pieces) are used for each square within a square.

There is another border, not easily distinguishable, in Colour A, with mitred corners. Make up the strips as in the cutting guide (use the four shorter strips). Attach these to the main section.

Make an eight-pointed star border, using templates 4, 10, 11, 12 and 13 – add ¼in (6mm) for seam allowances. This border has four matching stars for the corners, and 28 random-coloured stars, seven each side. Each star is made up of two colours. Use template 4 to cut the pieces from the fabric to make the stars. Colour A patchwork pieces form the background (see the photograph opposite). Use templates 10, 11, 12 and 13 to cut these pieces. Attach this border to the main section.

Make another border in Colour A (see cutting guide), mitring the corners. Attach this to the main section.

Make the final border. There are 176 geese in this border, and 16 squares within squares, this time at all the corners, halfway along each side and also a quarter-way along each side (see the photograph opposite for directions of "geese"). Attach this border to the main section.

Join the wadding strips. Tack the wadding and the lining to the quilt top. Place the quilt on a large quilting frame. Mark where you wish to quilt. This particular quilt was quilted with a pattern in the middle circle of the mariner's compass, around the outside of the points of the star to make a circle, inside the first border, on the plain triangles inside the second border, across the plain borders in a trellis pattern and around the patchwork on the patterned borders.

Bring the lining around to the front to edge the quilt, turning under the seam allowances.

Materials (cont.)

Colour C: 30in × 36in (77cm × 90cm) cotton.
Colour D: 30in × 36in (77cm × 90cm) cotton.
Colour E: 36in × 36in (90cm × 90cm) cotton.
Colour F: 90in × 90in (228cm × 228cm) polyester cotton sheeting.
Strips of patterned fabrics.
252in × 37in (640cm × 94cm) Terylene wadding.

Cutting guide

Colour A: 1 19¾in (50cm) square (½in (1.25cm) seam allowances included); 4 triangles (see *How to work*); 8 strips: 4 77in × 7½in (195.5cm × 19cm), and 4 50in × 7½in (127cm × 19cm) (½in/1.25cm seam allowances included); 1 piece from template 9, 8 from 5, 64 from 10, 36 from 11, 56 from 12, 8 from 13 (4 right way up, 4 *in reverse*).
Colour B: 8 pieces from template 1.
Colour C: 8 pieces from template 2.
Colour D: 16 pieces from template 3.
Colour E: 4 strips 21¼in × 1¼in (54cm × 3cm) plus ¼in (6mm) seam allowances.
Colour F: lining to finished size of quilt plus 3in (7.5cm) for edging and seam allowances.
From patterned fabrics: 248 pieces from template 6; 496 from 7 (at least 2 each fabric), 96 from 7 (all same fabric); 24 from 8 (all same fabric); 256 from 4 (28 of one fabric, 28 of one fabric, at least 7 of other fabrics).
Wadding (in strips if necessary) slightly larger than quilt.

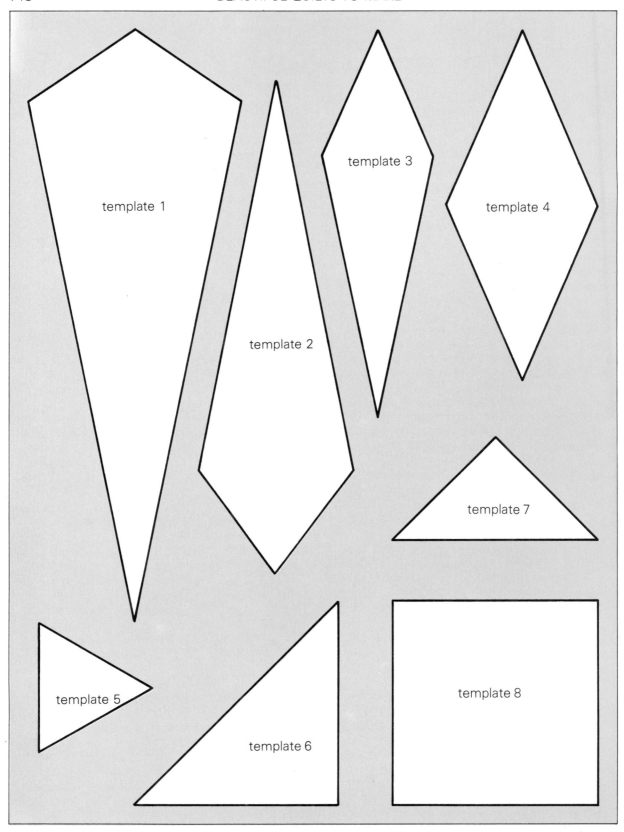

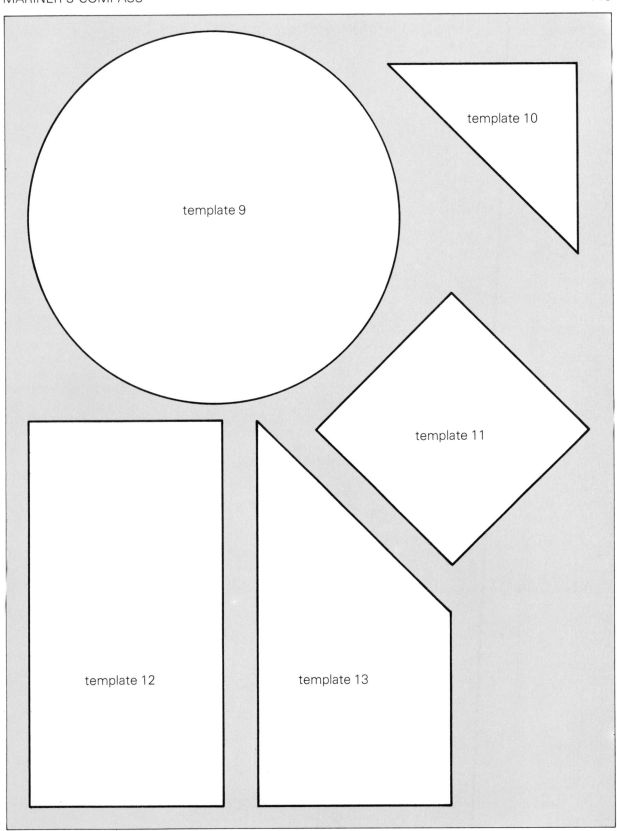

template 9

template 10

template 11

template 12

template 13

Cathedral window

Dimensions
41in × 32in (104cm × 81cm).

Materials
Colour A: 96in × 45in (244cm × 115cm) cotton.
Colour B: 77in × 45in (196cm × 115cm) cotton.
Colour C: 50in × 45in (127cm × 115cm) cotton.
Colour D: 48in × 36in (120cm × 92cm) polyester cotton (for lining).
44in × 37in (112cm × 94cm) Terylene wadding.

Cutting guide
Colour A: 63 6½in (16.5cm) squares plus ¼in (6mm) seam allowances; 36 half-squares plus ¼in (6mm) seam allowances for edges of quilt; 3in (7.5cm)-wide strips plus ¼in (6mm) seam allowances for edging frill.
Colour B: 70 surface squares plus ¼in (6mm) seam allowances.
Colour C: 28 surface squares plus ¼in (6mm) seam allowances; 1in (2.5cm)-wide strips for frame around main section of quilt.
Colour D: lining to size of finished quilt plus 1in (2.5cm) seam allowances.
Wadding slightly larger than quilt.

One WI member made this quilt on her own. She used different shades of blue for the cathedral window patchwork. The quilt was quilted by machine. A band of dark blue was appliquéd to the main section of the quilt and a frill was attached around the edges. The quilt is cot-sized.

How to work
Make the foundation squares in Colour A. (The technique for "cathedral window" patchwork is given on page 92.) The foundation squares are set on the diagonal so that they appear as diamond shapes. There are nine down and seven across. Make half-squares to fill in the gaps at the edges.

Make the surface squares in Colours B and C. These are attached to the foundation squares in an overall design that is based on the square diamond shape. Sixteen squares in Colour B form the centre of the diamond and they are edged with a band of twenty squares in Colour C. Around this shape, on the foundation squares, appliqué the narrow binding in Colour C so that a "frame" is made. Fill in the rest of the main section within this frame and outside it with squares in Colour B except for the two foundation squares in the corners of the frame, where two squares in Colour C are attached.

Join the wadding together. Tack the wadding and the lining to the quilt top. This particular quilt was quilted on the reverse by machine. If you decide to adopt this idea, remember that you will need to add extra lining to your material requirements. Slip-stitch and knot together the lining and the quilt top when you have finished quilting.

Attach the strips in Colour A, doubled, to the edge of the quilt, pleated in a frill.

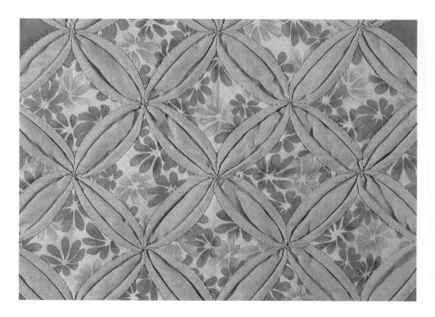

Close-up of the quilt opposite.

Cathedral window quilt made by Tegfan WI, Isle of Anglesey.

Samplers

When making a group quilt, tell everyone how many stitches per inch to quilt, so that the finished quilt will have overall uniformity.

Sampler quilts are excellent group projects because everyone can make a block to suit their ability and quilt it at home. When making a group quilt in this way, it is best to allow plenty of extra wadding in each block to avoid having to join it in the middle of a lattice, which can produce a ridge.

The quilt below is made up of twenty 12in (30cm) blocks, and it includes examples of hand-piecing, machine-piecing and appliqué. It also demonstrates the use of several different shapes, such as squares, triangles, hexagons, diamonds and curved seams. The blocks are traditional American ones, but there is also an original block by Marchwood WI, based on the WI logo.

The magnificent sampler quilt on the right is just as varied in its demonstration of different types of patchwork including clamshell, hexagons, and block patchwork, and the techniques for making them all are described elsewhere in this book.

Sampler quilt made by Marchwood WI, Hampshire.

Sampler quilt made by Bishopstone-with-Hinton Parva WI, Wiltshire.

Quilt by Bunny and Bradmore WI, Nottinghamshire.

Two original designs

The striking design of the quilt on the left is based on that of some small windows seen in Buckfast Abbey, Devon, by the designer, Inez Munton.

The quilt is made up of two different blocks, surrounded by an inner and an outer border, with outside triangles added as a finishing touch. It was made by a group of sixteen people of varying skills, using the template method.

The group quilt below, in more traditional style, was designed by Eleanor Allitt and was made by a group of eleven people.

This quilt is by the Kenilworth Quilters and its making is described in detail in chapter four. It has patchwork blocks interspersed with plain-coloured quilted blocks, which were especially dyed so that they harmonize with one another.

Acknowledgements

The editor would like to thank the following co-ordinators for their invaluable help with the technical details of the WI quilts in chapter seven. They are Christine Smith, Christine Clark, Barbara Kennaugh, Helen Wiseman, Yvonne Hayward, Sheila Kingsmill, Sheila Fox, Nina Rogers, Bonnie Kramrisch, Christine Salter, Isabel Sewell, Dorothy Thomas, Eileen Nuttall, Peggy Adams, Margaret Brown, Betty Ayre, June Smith, Molly Hunter, Yvonne O'Shaughnessy, Inez Munton and Joan Thompson

Our thanks to go to WI members, several of whom are also members of the Quilters' Guild: Valerie Ibbett, Pamela Allen, Brenda Marchbank, Barbara Keeling, Norah Barnes and Muriel Tooby, who lent items for photography, and to the following members of the Quilters' Guild for allowing us to use photographs of their work: Deirdre Amsden, Sheila Yale, Pamela Dempster, Jean Gage, Janet Wolchover, Isabel Dibden, Sheila Wilkinson, Ann Farmer, Jackie Curtis, Anthea Linacre, Jane Walmsley and Eleanor Allitt.

Our special thanks go to Brenda Cox, PRO of the Quilters' Guild, for her patient help and co-operation, and for allowing us to use a photograph of her quilt. Our thanks also to Jane Priestland, of the Stable Door, Langharne for lending us her old Welsh quilts for photography; to Mrs Diane Goodkind for allowing us to photograph Deirdre Amsden's quilt; to the Guildford Quilters for lending us their clamshell quilt; to the Kenilworth Quilters, whose group quilt is seen in chapter four; and to Marjorie Abraham for permission to reproduce the photo of the American group quilt on page 75, made by the Port Townsend Quilters.

The editor also wishes to acknowledge the following authors and publishers whose works proved to be a useful source of information during the preparation of this book: *The Perfect Patchwork Primer*, Beth Gutcheon (Penguin Books); *Discovering Patchwork*, Rosamund Richardson and Erica Griffiths (BBC Publications); *Good Housekeeping Quilting and Patchwork*, ed. Melanie Miller (Ebury Press); *Quilting*, Moyra McNeill (Octopus); *Patchwork*, Helen Fairfield (Octopus); *Patchwork Patterns*, Jinny Beyer (Bell & Hyman); *Patchwork*, Averil Colby (Batsford); *Quilts and Coverlets from the American Museum in Britain*, Sheila Betterton (The American Museum); *Patchwork and Appliqué*, Pamela Tubby (Cavendish House), and many other inspiring books on patchwork and quilting, including those published by Sterling, Bell & Hyman, E. P. Dutton and Ondorisha, to name but a few.

Index

Note: Numbers in italics refer to illustrations or photographs.

Aldbourne WI, work by, *142*
Allen, Pamela, work by, *109, 117*
Allitt, Eleanor, work by, *18, 24-5, 27, 155*
America, block patterns from, *see* block patchwork; *see also* American quilts, United States
American quilts, early, 6-7, 10, 26, 64, 80, 88
Amish quilts, 102, *102*
appliqué, 6, 40, 64-71;
   appliqué *perse*, 64;
   applying the shapes, 67, *67*;
   designing for, 66;
   equipment for, 67;
   examples of, *106, 108-9, 110, 133, 152*;
   fabrics for, 67;
   history of, 64;
   quilts, 64;
   templates for, *68-71*;
   see also clamshell, machine-appliqué

baby blocks design, 14-15, *14*, 19, *39, 110*
back stitch, 37, 63, *115*, 125
Baden Powell quilting design, *59*
bag,
   patchwork, *108, 110*;
   quilted, *115*
Barnes, Norah, work by, *114*
barn-raising design, 19, 88
basket of flowers design, 64;
   see also flower basket
batting, *see* wadding
bear's paw pattern, *22*
bed, measuring for a quilt, 10, 20, 23, 74
bedcovers, 6, 10-11, 20, 40, 42, 46;
   binding, 77, *76-7*;
   care and cleaning of, 79;
   cutting and sewing, 82-3 *82-3*;
   early American, *see* American;
   eighteenth-century, 6, 44;
   estimating quantities for, 74, 83;
   joining and finishing, 76-7, 84-5, *84-5*;
   lining, 76-7, 85, 88;

making, 72-85, 120-155, *120-155*;
   piping, 77;
   planning, 80-81, *81*, 82-3, *82-3*;
   see also bed, cot, group quilting
"bees", quilting, *see* group quilting
belt,
   patchwork, *109*;
   quilted, *115*
bias
   binding, 99, 134, 143;
   strips, 77, 122
Billington & Langho WI, work by, *138*
binding edges and corners, *76-7*, 77, 99, 122, 125
bird pictures quilt, 137-9, *137-9*
biscuit patchwork, *see* puff patchwork
Bishopstone-with-Hinton Parva WI, work by, *153*
block patterns, 12, 19, 20-1, *20-1*, 74, *80-1*, 81, 102, *110, 117, 122-4*, 125-7, *126-7*, 134-6, *134-6*, *137*, 152-3, *152-3, 155*;
   sewing, 37, 76;
   see also log cabin
borders, appliqué, 64;
   patchwork, 13, *13*, 20, 23, *23*, 74, 81, *81*, 83, 85, 101, 102, 146-7;
   quilting, 50, *52-3, 54, 56*
brick wall design, 17;
   variation of, *17*
Brockham Green WI, work by, *96*
Bullen, Jenny, work by, *43*
Bunny & Bradmore WI, work by, *154*, 155
butterfly quilting design, *54*
buttonhole stitch, 67

cable quilting design, *52*
calico,
   unbleached, 26;
   as lining, 46
carbon paper, dressmaker's, 47, 60, 88
cardboard templates, *see* templates
cathedral window patchwork, 7, *90-1*, 92-3, *107, 108, 110, 115, 117*, 150-1, *150-1*
cats and mice pattern, *22*
chalk pencil, dressmaker's, 47
chintz, 10, 30, 64;
   glazed cotton, 120;

quilt, 120-1, *120-1*
Christmas
   box, patchwork, *116*;
   cards, quilted, *112*;
   stocking, patchwork, *110*;
   tree decorations, patchwork, *116-7*;
   tree wall-hanging, *116*
church window (template), *32*
churn dash design, *21*
circle,
   quilting design, *52*;
   segments of (templates), *34*
clamshell
   patchwork, 94-5, *94-5, 108*, 152, *153*;
   quilting design, *55, 59*
cleaning quilts, 79;
   see also washing
clothing, made of patchwork, 6-7, 42, 44, 100, *109*
coffin (template), *32*
colour,
   use of and colour schemes, 7, 8-27, 47, 74, *80*, 81, *82*, 83;
   combinations, 26;
   families, 24-5;
   wheel, *25*;
   in Amish quilts, 102;
   in appliqué quilts, 64
colourfastness, 10, 30, 46, 79, 83, 130
Copthorne WI, work by, *65*
cord,
   for decoration, *113*;
   for piping and edging, 77, *77, 108, 110, 116*
cord and tassel quilting design, *57*
corded quilting, 42
corners, mitred, *76-7*
cot cover/quilt, *63*, 74, 130-3, *130-3*, 144-5, *144-5*, 150-1, *150-1*
cotton (fabric), 6-7, 30, 45, 88, 93, 98;
   cotton-polyester, 46, 120, 122, 143, 144, 147;
   domette, 46;
   for bedcovers, 74, 79, 130;
   lightweight, 67;
   printed, 64, 125;
   sheeting, 46;
   see also wadding
County Durham,
   quilting of, 42, 44;
courthouse steps design (log cabin), 19, 91, *91*
cowslip leaf quilting design, *54*

crazy patchwork, 6, 103, *103, 117*
creasing, crease-resistance, 30, 46
cross stitch, 67
cubes, *see* baby blocks design
Cuddington WI, work by, *123-4*
Curtis, Jackie, work by, *101*
cushions, 10;
    appliqué, *66, 106, 108*;
    patchwork, *107, 108*
cutting patches, 30, 36-7, 46;
    paper templates, 36, 46;
    threads, 46

decoration, *see* appliqué,
    Christmas, embroidery,
    quilting, stitches
Dempster, Pamela, work by, *31*
design of quilts, 7, 8-27, 50-1, 66,
    80-1, 81, 82-3, *82-3*, 88-91, *88-91*,
    102, 144;
    abstract composition, 10, *112-3*;
    for appliqué, *106*
diamonds, 12-13, 14-15, *14-15*,
    16-17, *16*, 19, 26, 31, *32, 107,
    110*, 140-1, *140*, 150, 152;
    see also lozenges
Dibden, Isabel, work by, *78*
double wedding ring quilt, 130-3,
    130-3
Dresden plate design, *117*, 122-4,
dressmaker's
    carbon paper, 47, 60, 88;
    pencil, see chalk
dry-cleaning quilts, 79, 106;
    see also washing
Durham, *see* County Durham
dyeing fabrics, 25, 26, 83, 155

edges,
    binding, 77, 85;
    quilting, 77;
    see also borders, raw edges,
    selvedges
Edwardian patchwork, 6
eighteenth-century patchwork, 6;
    Amish, 102;
    appliqué, 64
embroidery, 76, 85, *108*, 140;
    see also machine embroidery
embroidery hoop, 48, *48*
"English" patchwork, 6, 12, 72, 94,
    137;
    joining pieces together, 39, *39,*
    130, *133*
enlarging patterns or designs, 31,
    50-1, *50*
equilateral triangle, 14, 16, *16, 33*;
    see also lozenges
equipment
    for appliqué, 67;

for patchwork, 30-1;
    for quilting, 46-7, 48-9, *48*

fan,
    patchwork pattern, *134-5, 136*;
    quilting design, *52*;
    see also Dresden plate,
    grandmother's fan
Farmer, Ann, work by, *106*
feather quilting design, *53*;
    feather hammock, *53*
feather stitch, 67, 103
fabric, choice of, 10, 30, 46, 67, 74
filler quilting designs, 60, *60*
floral fabric, 120-1, *120-1*, 125, *126-7*
Florida, Seminole Indians of, 100
flower basket design, 20, *20*
flowers,
    formalized, 42;
    garlands of, 64;
    see also floral fabric
flying geese design (border), *146*,
    147
folded stars patchwork, 98-9, *98-9,
    114, 117*, 142-3, *142-3*
frame, quilting, 6, 48-9, *48*, 85, 134,
    146-7
frills, 74, 150

Gage, Jean, work by, *61*
geometric designs and shapes, 10,
    12-16, *12-16*, 20-3, *20-3*, 26, 50, 66
goose flight patchwork design, 88;
    see also flying geese
goose tail quilting design, *51*
goose wing quilting design, *55*
grandmother's cross block pattern,
    125-7, *126-7*
grandmother's fan quilt, 134-6,
    134-6
grandmother's flower garden, 13,
    13, 144, *144*
graph paper, use of in design, 12-14,
    31, 36, 50, 66, 74, *80*, 81, 88
grid (in block patterns), 20-1, *21-2*
group quilting, 6-7, 10, 48, *75*, 78, 80-
    5, *80-5*, 152, *155*
Guildford quilters, work by, *95*

hammock quilting design, *see*
    feather
hand-sewing
    appliqué, 67, *67;*
    cathedral window, 93, *93*;
    patchwork, 36-9, *37-8, 107-8,
    111-2, 114, 116-7*, 152;
    quilting, 48-9, 62-3, 110, *111-3,
    115-7*, 143
handy Andy pattern, *22*
heart quilting design, *56, 59*
hems, making, *67*
hens and chickens pattern, *22*

herringbone stitch, 76, 103
hexagons, 12-17, *12-13, 15*, 31, *32,
    107-8, 110, 114*, 120-1, *120-1*, 144,
    144-5, 152, *153*;
    see also rosette
history of
    appliqué, 64;
    patchwork, 6-7;
    quilting, 42, 44-5
hoop, quilting, 48-9, *48*

Ibbett, Valerie, work by, *92, 107,
    109, 114*
Imperial measurements, 7
interlining, 115, 120
ironing, *see* pressing
iron-on bonding, 67
iron-on patchwork patterns, 7
irregular pentagon, *33*
isometric graph paper, 13-14, 31
isosceles triangle, 16, *33*

Jacob's ladder design, *21*
joining blocks together, 37, 85, *84-5*

Keeling, Barbara, work by, *114, 116*
Kenilworth quilters, work by, *155*
knot quilting design, *55*
knotting, in quilting, 42, 47, 63, *63*,
    76, 120, 137

ladder stitch, 76, 85, 122
Lancaster County, quilt from, *102*
lattices, 20, 23, *23*, 74, 76, 81, 83, 85,
    125, *127*, 134
laundering, *see* washing
leaf, quilting design, *53-4, 58*
lettering, as a motif, 50
Linacre, Anthea, work by, *108, 110,
    115-6*
linen, 30, 46
lining fabric, 7, 46, 49;
    for bedcovers, 76-7, 85, 120
Llanfoist WI, work by, *135*
log cabin patchwork, 7, 19, 88-91,
    88-91, 102, *117*
Long, Bridget, work by, *109-10, 114*
lozenge, 13, *13*, 14, *14*, 144, *144*

machine appliqué, 67, 106, *109*
machine embroidery, *112*
machine patchwork,
    cathedral window, 92-3, *92-3*;
    crazy, 103;
    pieced, *109*, 152;
    puff, 97, *97*;
    Seminole, 100-1, *100-1*;
    strip, *109*
machine quilting, 46, 49, 62-3, 106,
    115, 140, 150

machine-sewing and machine-stitching, 26, 30, 37, 39, 76, 88, 110, 143
Marchbank, Brenda, work by, *112-3, 115*
Marchwood WI, work by, *152*
mariner's compass quilt, 146-9, *146, 148-9*
measurements, 7, 10, 74
medallion quilt, *31,* 64, 146
metal templates, *see* templates
metric measurements, 7
mitred corners, *76-7,* 125
motifs, 23, 50, 60, 64, 67
Munton, Inez, work by, *154,* 155
museums and patchwork or quilting, 10, 42, 51, 79, 103

needlecase, patchwork, *114*
needles, 30, 46-7, 83
New World settlers, 6-7 *see also* American quilts
nine-patch design, *21*

ocean wave pattern (hexagons), 13, *13*
octagons, 14, 17, *33, 110-1*
Old Catton (Evening) WI, work by, *129*
old maid's puzzle design, *21*
Onchan WI, work by, *126*

padding, 6;
    see also wadding
paisley pear quilting design, *51*
paper templates, *see* templates
parallelogram, *see* rhomboid
pastel pencil, 47
patches,
    cutting out, 36-7;
    joining together, 37, *37,* 38-9, *38-9,* 85, *84-5*
patchwork, *see* America, appliqué, bedcovers, block patterns, colour, clothing, design, "English", equipment, history, patches, patterns, quilting, sewing, small items, techniques, templates, *et passim*
patterns,
    patchwork, 14-17, *14-17,* 20-3, *20-3,* 32-5, *32-5,* 122-155; *122-155,*
    see also block patterns;
    quilting, 44-5, *44-5,* 50-60, *51-60, 124, 134;*
    see also templates
pear quilting design, *see* paisley, Welsh
pencil, use of in design, 19, 30, 47, 60, 83;

see also chalk, pastel
Pennsylvania, 102
pentagon, *34, 107;*
    irregular, *33, 114*
pieced patchwork, *see* "English" patchwork
pin cushion, *92, 107, 110, 114*
pineapple pattern (log cabin), 91, *91*
pinning,
    in appliqué, 67, *67;*
    in patchwork, 83, *84,* 85, 94, *94;*
    in quilting, 49, 63
pinwheels design, *21*
piping, 26, 77, *77,* 130
plait quilting design, *56*
plaited block patchwork design, *110*
planning patchwork, *see* design
plastic templates, *see* templates
polyester, *see* cotton
pressing patches, 37
Preston On Stour WI, work by, *39*
prickly pear pattern, *22*
puff patchwork, 96-7, *96-7*
purse, patchwork, *115*
pyramids design, 16, *16*

quantities, estimating, *see* bedcovers, measurements
quilt, *see* bedcover
quilters, modern, 26
quilting, 6-7, 26, 40-63, 85;
    and appliqué, *106;*
    edges, 77, 85;
    corded, 42, *115;*
    County Durham, 42;
    design of, 50-1;
    in the ditch, 42;
    Italian, 42, *115;*
    outline, 42;
    preparation of, 49;
    shadow, 42;
    thread, *see* thread;
    traditional, 44-5, *44-5;*
    Trapunto, 42;
    Welsh, 42, 44-5, *44-5;*
    see also "bees", design, equipment, frames, group quilting, hand-sewing, machine-quilting, patterns, stitches

raw edges, 26, 67, 103
rectangle, 16-17, *17,* 20, 23, 31, *110;*
    adapted, *34;*
red blocks quilt, 140-1, *140-1*
reducing patterns, 51
rhomboid, 15-16, *16,* 19, *34;*
    parallelogram, 17
ribbon, 26, 98, *107*
rose quilting design, *55, 57*

rosette (of hexagons), 13, *13, 110*
round the twist design, *110*
roundels, *see* folded stars
running stitch, 62, 77, *115,* 125, 140

Salt Lake City design, 137
sampler quilts, 152, *152-3*
sandpaper, *see* templates
sashings, *see* lattices
satin, 106, *106, 114*
satin stitch, 67, 103
scallop quilting design, *54*
scalloped edge, 122
scraps, in patchwork, 6, 10, 103, *103,* 120
sea horse, appliqué design, *106*
seam allowances,
    general note, 7;
    for appliqué pieces, 67;
    for bedcovers, 74;
    for block patchwork pieces, 37, 81, 85
seams, 37, *37,* 39, 62;
    butted, 125;
    curved, 152
selvedges, 74
Seminole patchwork, 100-1, *100-1, 117*
sewing
    appliqué, 67, *67;*
    patchwork, 36-9, *37-9;*
    see also hand-sewing, machine-sewing, machine-quilting, stitches
sewing thread, *see* thread
shapes, choosing, 12-19
    see also design
shell,
    appliqué design, *106;*
    quilting design, *55*
Shenstone WI, work by, *145*
Shipton Oliffe WI, work by, *11*
shrinkage of fabrics, 30, 83, 130
silk, 30, 46, 79, *108, 110, 115*
size of bedcover, *see* bed, bedcover
sky rocket pattern, *22*
slip stitch, 94, 122
small items of patchwork and quilting, 104-117, *106-117*
Somerset patchwork, *see* folded stars
Southwell WI, work by, *131*
spectacle case, *110*
spiral, 45;
    quilting design, *55*
splicing cord for piping, 77
spraying (dyes), 26
squared paper, 19, 20, 23, 66
squares, 16-17, *16-17,* 23, 31, *110-1,* 147, 152;
    see also block patterns
squat diamonds, 16-17, *16*

star of Bethlehem design, 15
stars, 15, *15*, *108*, *110*, *112*, *116-7*, 147;
  of hexagons, *144*;
  template, *35*;
  see also folded stars
stencilling, 26
stencil paper, see templates
"stepping" a join, 76, *76*
stitches,
  appliqué, 67;
  parallel lines of, 62;
  quilting, 42, 45, *44-5*, 49, 62;
  see also back stitch, embroidery, hand-sewing, herringbone, ladder, machine-sewing, running, tacking
Stoke Fleming WI, work by, *120-1*
storage of quilts, 79
straight edge (hexagons), *13*
straight furrow design, 88
strip
  binding, 77;
  patchwork, 72, *109*, *117*
striped fabric, 140
stuffed quilting, 42
Suffolk puff patchwork, 97, *97*, *112*
synthetic fabrics, see fabric, wadding

tacking, 30, 48-9, 62, 67, 77, 83, 85, 98-9, *98-9*
Tadworth WI, work by, *63*
tea cozy, *108*
techniques,
  appliqué, 64, 66-7, *67*;
  finishing, 76-7, *76-7*;
  patchwork, 28-39, *32-9*, 80-5, *80-5*, 92-103, *92-103*;
  quilting, 40-51, *50-1*, 60-3, *60*, *63*
Tegfan WI, work by, *151*
templates for appliqué, 66-7, *67*, *68-71*
templates, for patchwork, 7, 31, *32-5*;
  cardboard, 30-1, 36, 81, *81*, 88, *88*, 94, 116, 125;
  diamond, *32*, *140*;
  fabric, 30, *36*, 130;
  hexagon, *32*, *120*, *144*;
  metal, 31;
  paper, 30, 36, *36*, 37-8, 46, *82*, 83, 85, 114, 128, 130, 144;
  plastic, 31;
  stencil paper, 31;
  triangle, 83, *127-8*;
  window, 31, 36-7, *36*, 74, *82*, 137
templates for quilting, 47, 50-1, *51-9*, 60
Terylene wadding, 7, 122, 125
thimble, 30, 47;

  -holder, *107*;
  leather, 42, 47
thread,
  -holder, *114*;
  linen, 63, 137;
  quilting, 47, 85, 114;
  sewing, 30, 83
three-dimensional designs, 14, *14-15*, 88, 140, *141*
tie-quilting, 47
tone (in design), 10, 14-20, *18-19*, 23, 26, 81
Tooby, Muriel, work by, *18*
tracing
  designs, 32, 50-1, 60, 66-7;
  wheel, 60, 88
traditonal quilting and patchwork, 20, *44-5*, 88, *152-3*
transferring patterns, 60
trapezoid, *34*, *110*
Trapunto quilting, 42
trellis quilting pattern, 147
triangle, 14-17, *14*, *16*, 20, 23, 33, *107*, *110-2*, *127-8*, 128, 147, 152
tumbling blocks design, 14, *14*;
  see also baby blocks
Turkey red, 26
tying (in quilting), see knotting

United States of America, 6;
  see also America, New World
Upchurch WI, work by, *90*

variable star design, *21*
velvet, *108*, 115
Victorian patchwork, 6, 103

wadding, 7;
  cotton, 46, 60, 79;
  joining strips of, 76, *76*;
  machining onto, 109;
  polyester, 46;
  in puff patchwork, 97, *97*;
  for quilting, 49, 85, 115;
  synthetic, 42, 46, 60;
  wool, 45;
  see also Terylene
waistcoat, patchwork, *109*
Wales, quilting in, 42, 44-5, *44-5*, 80
wall-hangings, 10, *18*, *24*, *43*, 78-9, *78*, *109*, *111*, *116*
Walmsley, Jane, work by, *107*, *111*, *114*
washing fabrics and quilts, 30, 46, 79, 83
wedding quilt, 64
Welsh pear quilting design, *56*
white, use of as a colour, 26
wide-angled shapes, sewing, *38*
Wilkinson, Sheila, work by, *109*
window templates, see templates
Wolchover, Janet, work by, *66*

Women's Institutes, 7, 80, 118;
  work by, *39*, *63-5*, *90*, *96*, *98*, *120-1*, *123*, *126*, *129*, *131*, *135*, *138*, *141*, *143-6*, *151-4*
wool, 26, 46, 79, 115;
  see also wadding

zigzag
  border, 120;
  patterns (block patchwork), 17, *17*, 128-9, *128-9*;
  stitch, 37, 67, 103